Bernard J. McGuckian S.J.

GW00393402

Pledged For Life

To Mary
with best wishes

Fr Barney sj.

Dunlery 20/10/01

Pioneer Total Abstinence Association of the Sacred Heart

First Published 1997
Second Edition 1998

Nihil Obstat:
Tim Hamilton S.J.
Censor Deputatus

Imprimi Potest:
+ Desmond, Archbishop of Dublin,
Primate of Ireland.

Origination:
Crotare

Printing
Gen Print, Dublin

ISBN 0 9531151 0 0

Published by Pioneer Publications, Dublin.
27 Upper Sherrard Street, Dublin 1, Ireland.
Telephone: (01) 8749464.   Fax: (01) 8748485
E-Mail: pioneer@clubi.ie
Website: http://www.clubi.ie/pioneer/

*To my mother who would be
happy with even the feeblest
efforts to honour the
Sacred Heart and the
memory of my father who
entered into the arms of
His tender mercy
thirty years ago*

Pledged For Life

Contents

Section One:
Spirituality of the Association

Section Two:
Organisational Procedures

Foreword

The Pioneer commitment is clear, unambiguous and twofold: to pray the heroic offering daily and to abstain from alcohol for life. Its inspiration is clearly from Jesus Christ himself. Asked by his disciples why they could not exorcise a possessed boy, Jesus said: "This kind can be cast out only by prayer and fasting" (Mark 9:27, 28). What the founder of the Pioneer Association, Fr. James Cullen, SJ., launched on 28th December 1898 was nothing less than a campaign of prayer and fasting to combat the demon of alcohol abuse.

The essence of the Pioneer Association lies in devotion to the person of Christ expressed in living the pledges of the heroic offering which is addressed to the Sacred Heart of Jesus. Devotion to the Sacred Heart is of course much wider than the Pioneer Association. For that reason I feel certain that this attractive book, *Pledged for Life,* will appeal to very many beyond the boundaries of the Association.

This is a delightful compilation covering the history of the Association and of devotion to the Sacred Heart, reflections on the heroic offering, what the Scriptures say about the motivation underlying the Pioneer Movement, Our Lady in Pioneer spirituality, young people in the Pioneer Movement, prayers, hymns, and much more.

Pledged for Life, complements *Toward a Second Century,* the definitive work on the Pioneer Association published in 1993. Both publications are very timely. In 1998-99 we celebrate the centenary of the Pioneer Association; and, as we approach the new millennium, there is a growing awareness worldwide of the need to address the use and abuse of alcohol. Recently the European Region of the World Health Organisation, embracing some 850 million people, adopted a new European Alcohol Action Plan designed to combat "a problem that for generations has been taken for an unavoidable curse that societies just had to endure" (*Alcohol - Less is Better:* Report of the WHO European Conference on Health, Society and Alcohol, December 1995, p.5)

Dr. Thomas A. Finnegan
Bishop of Killala

Acknowledgements

I wish to thank Archbishop Michael Neary, Fr Michael Campbell, Fr Daniel Dargan, Fr Leon Ó Morcháin, Sister Michael, S.M., and Br Kevin Treacy C.B., all members of the Spirituality Committee of the Pioneer Association for their encouragement. They felt that there was a need to complement the principal contemporary document of the Association, *Toward a Second Century,* with something akin to an inspirational handbook for members. They envisaged it as a help to those with practical responsibility for conducting meetings, organising liturgical functions and giving talks. At the same time, it should help all those interested in Sacred Heart devotion. Again it should serve as an introduction to the spirituality of the Pioneer Association. Working on the assumption that a camel is a horse designed by a committee the members of our small group decided it best that one of us put the work together. The lot fell to me. I must take responsibility for what appears except where it is obvious that the material has its source elsewhere.

My brothers in the Society of Jesus have made it possible for me to give myself full time to promoting Sacred Heart Devotion. One of them, Ray Lawler has done his best to ensure that this production is word perfect. If it is not, the fault is mine. Maureen Manning, Roísín Fulham, Angela Clyne, Bernadette Gismondi and Mary O'Luanaigh were as helpful in this as in all the other projects in which we involve ourselves at the Pioneer Central Office. Sr Camilla Roche IBVM offered invaluable advice on every aspect of the production. Liam Killion and Vivienne McGuinness showed their accustomed patience with my constant chopping and changing. I am most grateful to all of them.

Introduction

Members of the Pioneer Total Abstinence Association of the Sacred Heart of Jesus, popularly known as the Pioneers, abstain for life from intoxicating drink. The motivation for their choice is rooted in Catholic spirituality. In this perspective, drink like everything else created is good. Evil is always derivative and only arises with the abuse of something good.

The Pioneer believes that moderation in drink is a good thing but to give it up for a high ideal is a better thing. This is a simple extension of the understanding of fasting in Christian tradition. To enjoy a good dinner each day of one's life, something unexceptionable, is the normal course of action for most of us. To freely forego this, out of love for God and the salvation of others, as did the Venerable Matt Talbot or the Servant of God, Father John Sullivan of the Society of Jesus, is something better. However, callings and graces differ so we have to discern where each of us is personally called.

In the Catholic tradition, temperance, one of the cardinal virtues, always meant restraint in the different pleasurable areas of life. It took the form appropriate to the area involved. Each one had to moderate the pleasures attaching to sexuality, food and intoxicating drink by exercising the appropriate virtues of chastity, abstinence and sobriety. During the 18th and 19th centuries in Northern Europe and North America this terminology was modified by Protestant social and moral reformers whose main concern was the abuse of intoxicating drink. Since the early days of the Reformation they had broken with the practice implied in "days of fast and abstinence". They retained the use of the word, abstinence, which had applied in the Catholic tradition to refraining from certain types of food but transferred it to cover drink. One significant result of their successful exertions was that in the English-speaking world the word, temperance, began to lose its more extensive meaning and was eventually reduced to mean extreme care in the use of intoxicating drink. This prepared the ground for acceptance by both Protestants and Catholics of the term "total abstinence" as meaning complete renunciation of intoxicating drink and produced what became known as the Temperance Movement.

Through the early decades of the 19th century the big debate within this movement, mainly confined to Protestantism, was the relative merits of moderation in the use of alcohol and total abstinence from it. The Total

Abstinence wing of the movement won the day with the result that, in popular perception, the terms temperance and total abstinence became synonymous. Catholicism only entered the fray late in the day. It was not until 1838 in Cork, under the inspiration of the great Capuchin friar Fr Theobold Mathew, that the practice of total abstinence first made significant headway in Catholicism. In his phenomenally successful campaigns in Ireland, Britain and North America, among people of all denominations, he accepted the terminology developed by the Protestant reformers and used it to great effect. By the time Fr Cullen came to found the Pioneers, "total abstinence" was universally used in the context of intoxicating drink and "taking the pledge" had become an established practice in Irish life.

Fr Cullen's main source of inspiration was the Scriptures. From his reading of I Corinthians 12, he concluded that we are all members of the Mystical Body of Christ, with the consequent responsibility for and indeed wonderful possibility of helping one another, even people we have never met. " Now Christ's body is yourselves, each of you with a part to play in the whole" (verse 27). From this he deduced that prayer and self-denial (along with almsgiving the three marks of genuine religion) offered to God for others could be of benefit to them. Other scripture passages highlight our capacity in God's providence to cooperate in the salvific work of Christ. The assertion, for instance, that "the life and death of each of us has its influence on others", (Romans 14:7) and the reminder that "this is a wicked age, but your lives should redeem it" (Eph:5,16) are all in line with Fr Cullen's overall interpretation of Christian revelation.

However what was most distinctive about the Pioneer way, in the mind of Fr Cullen, was the focus on Sacred Heart Devotion, as revealed to St Margaret Mary Alacoque at Paray-le-Monial. She had taught that three special benefits for the human family would follow from widespread devotion to the Sacred Heart: sinners would find an ocean of mercy, tepid souls would become fervent and the already fervent would rise quickly to great perfection. (cf. Appendix A) There would be a general uplifting of the quality of life. In Fr Cullen's own terms, people on different rungs of the ladder would benefit from the "pioneering" efforts of the Association. His main concern, however, was the pitiable victims of alcohol addiction and his great hope that "they (the Pioneers) would win from Heaven by the gentle violence of total abstinence the conversion of excessive drinkers".

In the following pages we try to outline and elaborate on some aspects of the spirituality which has underpinned this remarkable movement. The most authoritative document on this, as on all matters dealing with the Association, is *Toward a Second Century*, which this work is intended to complement. Essential to any appreciation of Pioneer motivation is an understanding of

Devotion to the Sacred Heart. For this reason a section deals with the history of Sacred Heart Devotion in the Catholic Church from the beginning but especially over the last three centuries. Fr Daniel Dargan, Central Director of the Association from 1953-75, shares his prayerful reflections on the "Heroic Offering", the prayer bequeathed by the founder and recited daily by members. A short selection has been made among the many thousands of talks given over the years at Pioneer events and published extensively in the public press, especially the *Irish Catholic* newspaper and the *Pioneer*, the monthly magazine and official organ of the association, in publication since 1948. These may be consulted in the Archives at University College Dublin where the voluminous records of the Association have recently been deposited. A short section deals with the lives of Pioneers whose causes for canonization are already underway. The main inspiration for the chapter on the use of wine in scripture is the writings of Xavier Leon-Defour S.J., the celebrated French exegete. Prayers, hymns, reflections and aids for the celebration of liturgical and para-liturgical functions which have proved helpful in the past have been incorporated to nourish the devotion of Pioneers and indeed others who may be well disposed.

Bernard J. McGuckian S.J.
Feast of the Sacred Heart, June 6th, 1997.

SECTION ONE: Spirituality of the Association

Chapter One

Devotion To The Sacred Heart through the Ages

*Devotion to the Sacred Heart is devotion
to the things closest to the Sacred Heart*
Fr Frederick Crowe SJ

IN THE CHURCH FROM THE BEGINNING

On October 17th, 1690 Saint Margaret Mary Alacoque died in the Visitation Monastery in Paray-le-Monial a small French town in the province of Burgundy. A few months earlier on July 12th, in a battle on the banks of the River Boyne, not far from the Irish town of Drogheda, William, the Protestant Prince of Orange defeated his father-in-law, James II, the Catholic and erstwhile King of England, thus copper-fastening religious differences that are still unhappily with us. The saint and the unsuccessful soldier-king had something else in common, besides the fact that in 1690 one died and the other was defeated. Both had a connection with St Claude la Colombière. It was at St James's Palace, the London residence of James, then Duke of York, that Claude first spoke publicly about the devotion to the Heart of Christ he had learned from Margaret Mary. He frequently preached about it in the Queen's Chapel at St James's before his banishment in 1679 from England where he had spent the previous three years as chaplain to James's second wife, Mary of Modena. Claude's death at Paray-le-Monial a few years later in 1682 as a result of tuberculosis contracted in a London prison ended his seven year friendship with Margaret Mary but not before they had set in train one of the great movements in Christian history. She was canonised in 1920 and Claude himself in 1992.

Margaret Mary anticipated a great flowering of Devotion to the Sacred Heart but, as she repeatedly told members of her community, it would only come after her death. It was yet another case of the need for the seed to fall into the ground and die if there was to be a harvest. One instance of this fruit has been the growth of religious life. In the three centuries since the death of the two friends, over 280 new religious orders, based on Devotion to the Sacred Heart and incorporating the term in their title, have come into the Church, about 150 of them in the 20th century alone. The Pioneer Association itself is an instance of this devotion applied to a social problem. This extraordinary force for good in contemporary society has its roots in the distant past, much further back than the century of Margaret Mary and Claude.

As natives of Eastern France these two saints were heirs to a long tradition of devotion to the Heart of Christ. There were traces of it in the teaching of St Irenaeus who was to that part of the world what St Patrick is to the Irish. A native of modern Turkey he made his way to Europe and was Bishop of Lyons before his death around the year 200 a.d. He could say "The Church is the fountain of living water that flows to us from the Heart of Christ". The witness of Irenaeus is of capital importance because he can be considered a sort of "second generation" believer. He had sat at the feet of Polycarp of Smyrna who in turn had actually seen the apostle John and had heard the words of life from John's own lips. Irenaeus, in talking about "living water" and its source, must have been influenced by the quotation from John's Gospel: "From his heart shall flow streams of living water" (7:38). But John in his turn was quoting from the Prophet Isaiah: "From his heart shall flow streams of living water", (55,3). Given this background it is not surprising that John is the only one of the evangelists to focus on the water that came from the side of Christ as soon as he was pierced with the lance. He saw this as the fulfillment of the ancient prophecies and as a promise of a future outpouring of the Spirit that would know no bounds.

On the night before he stood on Calvary and witnessed the piercing of the side of Jesus, John had rested his head on the Lord's breast. This privilege was highly appropriate for the "beloved disciple", nourishing his faith and enabling him to sound the depths of "wisdom and knowledge" in the Saviour's heart. The experience of this overwhelming love sustained him through the trauma that would prove too much for the others. Of those who shared the Last Supper, he alone did not run away. According to tradition John was the last of the apostles to die, living at Ephesus to be very old. Even when he was too old to walk and had to be carried to the gatherings of the believers, they kept trying to get him to go back into the recesses of his memory:

"Father John, was there not some other word that the Master said?" His invariable answer was "Little children, love one another". When some of them complained that he always said the same thing he replied. "I say the same thing because there is nothing else to say. This was the Master's only message."

A DEVOTION ROOTED IN SCRIPTURE

The Saviour's Heart in the Old Testament

Although the sufferings in the human heart of the God-man only took place during his days on earth, they were already anticipated in Old Testament prophecies. Hugo Rahner, the German Jesuit scholar, like his brother Karl, wrote extensively on Sacred Heart Devotion. When searching for Old Testament references to the Heart of the Saviour, he was very selective. A passage had to refer, not just in a general way to the heart of God but specifically to the suffering heart of the promised Messiah. Here are three passages which fulfil Rahner's demanding requirements.

The first is in Psalm 40(39) 7-9.

> *You wanted no sacrifice or cereal offering,*
> *but you gave me an open ear.*
> *You did not ask for burnt offering or sacrifice for sin*
> *then I said, 'Here I am,*
> *I am coming.*
> *In the scroll of the book it is written of me,*
> *My delight is to do your will;*
> *Your law, my God,*
> *is deep in my heart'*

Commenting on this passage, Rahner writes: "The Heart of the Messiah, around which God has formed a human body, is the innermost sanctum of the temple. There stands the altar of the sacrifice that redeemed the world".

The second is the choice of prayer of the Saviour as He was dying on the altar of sacrifice. Jesus was heard to cry out the first verse of Psalm 22(21), "My God, my God, why have you forsaken me?". The sound of these words in Aramaic, *Eli, eli, lama sabachthani,* caused the people standing around to misinterpret him as calling on Elijah. As a good Jew, he would have known the psalm by heart, but as the Messiah, he would have known that the stark reality of it was now being fulfilled to the letter in his own breaking heart:

> *Like water I am poured out*
> *disjointed are all my bones*
> *my heart has become like wax*
> *It is melted within my breast. (v.14)*

The opening words of this psalm are filled with distress but it ends in a great cry of hope, as Jesus knows that the sacrifice of his broken heart will be accepted by the Father and that his invitation issued at the Last Supper "to do this in remembrance of me" will not go unheeded.

"The whole wide world will remember and return to the Lord, all the families of nations bow down before him." (v. 27)

The third is St Peter's choice of text when he first preached in public after the Resurrection, as recorded in Acts 2, 30-31. Peter interpreted Psalm 16 (15) as a prophecy about the heart, soul and body of the Messiah. The suffering is now over and the glorification has begun:

> ***So my heart rejoices, my soul delights,***
> ***my body too will rest secure,***
> ***for you will not abandon me to Sheol***
> ***you cannot allow your faithful servant to see the abyss (v. 9-10)***

These and other Old Testament texts, especially those about the outpouring of a mysterious water, prepared the way for the great revelation about the outpouring of the Spirit that would be a gift to humanity from the Heart of the Saviour.

The Heart of Jesus in the New Testament

Bishop Sheen, in his usual imaginative way, said that the Old Testament was to the New Testament what radio was to television. In radio we could hear but we could not see. In T.V. we can both hear and see. John begins his First Letter by describing his own "hands on" experience of the Word Incarnate:

> *"Something which has existed since the beginning, which we have seen with our own eyes, which we have watched and touched with our own hands, the Word of life - this is our theme".*
>
> *I John 1.*

In this passage, John never once uses the word "heart", but surely what was being revealed to him and the others privileged to meet Jesus was his Heart. Pius XII wrote: "The Heart of our Redeemer is a living heart, endowed no less than ours with the power of feeling, throbbing with the manifold emotions and feelings of His soul, quivering with the burning love of His twofold will (human and divine). And if the Evangelists and the other Sacred Writers do not actually describe all this, they do nevertheless frequently set in their proper light this divine love and its concomitant emotions of the senses, that is to say desire, joy, sickness of heart, fear and anger, in so far as they are betrayed by his facial expression, his words and gestures. The countenance especially of our adorable Saviour was a token and indeed a mirror most faithful of the emotions which moved his soul in varying manner and, like a succession of waves, reached his Sacred Heart and set it throbbing to their rhythm". *(Haurietis Aquas, 1956).*

In his account of the life and death of Jesus, John uses a prophecy from Zechariah: "They will look on the one whom they have pierced". (12,10). A few verses later Zechariah spoke of a mysterious fountain that would appear one day. "When that day comes, a fountain will be opened for the House of David and the inhabitants of Jerusalem, to wash sin and impurity away" (13,1). In his use of an Old Testament text at this supreme moment in the life of Jesus, John saw the fulfilment of the words of Isaiah: "From his heart shall flow streams of living water".

In succeeding centuries men and women have been inspired to great holiness through their love for the Heart of Christ. In more modern times we have the extraordinary example of Blessed Damien of Molokai who committed himself so much to the care of lepers that he became one himself. He was beatified in 1995. The inspiration of his life was his love for the Sacred Heart.

THE DEVOTION TAKES SHAPE IN THE CHURCH

Devotion to Christ was born as soon as the first disciples began to feel the attraction of His personality. The experience warmed their hearts as it has those of millions ever since. Envious begrudgers found this unbearable. "The whole world has gone after him" they complained. (John 12,19). To prevent this they were prepared to go to any lengths, even crucifixion. But as he himself indicated, this would have a boomerang effect. "And when I am lifted up from the earth, I shall draw all peoples to myself" (John 12,32). Devotion is a response to this drawing power of Christ. "Real living devotion", as St Francis de Sales put it, "presupposes the love of God; is in fact that very love, although it has many aspects. In so far as this love adorns the soul and makes it pleasing to God, it is called grace, in so far as it empowers us to do good, it is called charity; when it is so perfect that it moves us, not merely to do good, but to do good carefully, frequently and readily, then it is called devotion" *(Introduction to the Devout Life).* The purpose of the reflection and preaching of the Fathers of the Church during the first thousand years of Christianity was to nourish devotion to the person of Christ.

John ends his gospel with this dramatic claim: "There was much else that Jesus did; if it were written down in detail, I do not suppose the world itself would hold all the books that would be written" (21, 25). In other words, the mystery of the Incarnation is infinite. Coming to terms with something so far beyond us has always been challenging but not impossible. St Bernard of Clairvaux approached it positively: "In the Incarnation, God stooped to the level of our imagination", he said. Through the centuries, believers felt justified in giving imaginative expression to their love for the Lord. They not only cherished in memory details of his life, death and resurrection but even found a place for the material objects connected with it. The thought of the Passion inspired them to heartfelt devotion and, by an association of ideas, the very wood of the cross itself took on a symbolic significance. Emperor Constantine's vision of the cross and accompanying words *"In hoc signo vinces"* (in this sign you shall conquer) must have contributed to this development in the Western Church as did the finding of the True Cross, traditionally attributed to St Helena, his mother. Again, the weapon used to pierce his side became known as the "Holy Lance". Anything that helped "earth" the mystery without being far-fetched usually received official church approval. Devotion, based on different aspects of his person, developed over the centuries. The Five Wounds became known as the Precious Wounds. Saint Catherine of Siena mentioned the Precious Blood in practically all her letters while the Holy Face had a special fascination for Saint Thérèse of Lisieux. All these devotions were a way of honouring the total mystery that was Christ.

One of the most important figures in this development was Saint Anselm of Canterbury, known to many theologians as the Father of Devotion to the Sacred Heart. He is one of the first mystics to stress the link between the wounded side and the loving heart: "The opening of the side of Christ reveals the riches of his love, the love of this Heart for us". He was soon joined by the great Cistercian, St Bernard of Clairvaux: "The secret of his Heart lies visible through the clefts of his Body; visible too the great mystery of his love, and the bowels of his mercy". The influence of Bernard, known as the last of the Fathers and Mellifluous Doctor, ensured a Sacred Heart dimension to all subsequent piety especially in the network of Cistercian monasteries, male and female, that spread out from Clairvaux in the 12th century and also among the Franciscans and the Dominicans, both orders founded in the early 13th century.

> The Church seems in a particular way to profess the mercy of God and to venerate it when she directs herself to the Heart of Christ. In fact, it is precisely this drawing close to Christ in the mystery of his Heart which enables us to dwell on this point - a point in a sense central and also most accessible on the human level- of the revelation of the merciful love of the Father, a revelation which constituted the central content of the messianic mission of the Son of Man.
>
> **Pope John Paul 11, Dives in Misericordia, Part 13. November 30th, 1980.**

FRANCISCAN AND DOMINICAN INFLUENCE

Early in the 13th century, devotion to the Heart of Christ, already firmly established in monasteries of the Benedictine tradition, received a whole new lease of life with the appearance of the Franciscans and Dominicans, the two new preaching orders founded around the same time. In the early days of his conversion St Francis heard a voice coming from the crucifix at the dilapidated church of St Damian saying, " Francis, go and repair My house, which you see is falling down." In his simplicity, Francis set about repairing the old building. Eventually he realised that it was the whole Church that was in need of "repair", a notion that would figure so prominently as "reparation" in subsequent devotion to the Heart of Christ. About that vision, Josef Stierli, a Swiss Jesuit, wrote:

"What touched Francis' heart so deeply was not simply the external suffering of Christ, but the Passion of his Heart; and the spirit of St. Francis has never ceased to direct his sons to the suffering Heart of Jesus". The greatest of his disciples, St Bonaventure, believed that the surest way to the Father is a burning love for the crucified Christ which only reaches perfection in a true union of hearts. Women of the Franciscan tradition like St Margaret of Cortona, the mistress of a rich landowner and mother of his child before her conversion, wanted to lose herself in the Heart of the Lord. She shared this desire with other Franciscans, especially St Angela of Foligno, like herself another convert from a life of public sin.

The fountain head of the Dominican tradition of Sacred Heart devotion was

St Albert the Great. His teaching influenced a galaxy of mystics of his Order: Meister Eckhart, John Tauler, Blessed Henry Suso and perhaps the greatest of them, the Dominican tertiary, St Catherine of Siena. In Albert's writing he insists that the streams of wisdom and knowledge flowing from the Heart of the Saviour are freely on offer to all believers. John the Apostle resting his head on the breast of the Lord is the model for all of us in this. Albert marvelled at how the institution of the Eucharist was a source of great joy to the Sacred Heart, "His heart overflowed with love and joy at being completely one with us and filling our hearts with joy and jubilation". This insistence on the connection between the Eucharist, especially the Precious Blood, and the Sacred Heart becomes a recurrent theme in Catherine of Siena. She repeatedly refers to the Precious Blood in practically all of her many letters. In 1370, on receiving the vision which resulted in an extraordinary exchange of hearts, known in mystical theology as "transverberation", Jesus made this consoling offer to Catherine: "Think of me, and I will unceasingly think of you". A similar occurrence is reported in the lives of both St Teresa of Avila and St Margaret Mary. All three received the "tranverberation", as well as an accompanying pain in the side which remained with them for the rest of their lives.

Perhaps the greatest flowering of Sacred Heart devotion in the Middle Ages took place in Germany, towards the end of the 13th century, in a monastery of Cistercian nuns at Helfta, near Eisleben in the east of the country. Of the many great women in this monastery two of the most outstanding were Blessed Mechtild of Hackeborn and St. Gertrude the Great. Three things helped them scale the heights of holiness; the solemn liturgy inherited from St Benedict, mystical love in the tradition of St Bernard and inspired spiritual direction from their Dominican neighbours. Both these women left written accounts of their intense spiritual experiences. In Mechtild's *Book of Special Graces*, the focus is not on the Man of Sorrows but on the Heart of the glorified Christ where she finds consolation, refuge and peace. This work, along with a number of very tender prayers to the Sacred Heart, profoundly influenced European piety. St Peter Canisius, the Apostle of Germany, was using them three centuries after her death. St Gertrude, generally regarded as the most outstanding of these great women, concentrated on the Heart of the Crucified Lord in her best-known work (many have been lost), *"The Ambassador of Divine Love"*. The workings of the Sacred Heart, as she presents them, are strikingly similar to what St Margaret Mary would report in a later age: "I have presented my Heart to you so often as a sign of our most constant love. Because of this, when you ask me for anything, point to my Heart, which I took for love of men in the Incarnation, and I will bestow on you from It the grace you ask me for".

As this intense devotion, carefully nurtured in the convents and monasteries, began to move out into general church life, it prompted the comment that " from the 13th to the 15th centuries the Franciscans and the Dominicans made all Europe weep". The theme of the heart featured prominently in the piety they popularised. Many poems and prayers from the period are still extant. With the approach of the 16th century, as some of the energy went out of the effort of the friars, it was the Carthusians who took over the lead in promoting the devotion. Their commitment to contemplative silence, solitude and vicarious suffering for others opened them to the great possibilities for spiritual growth in the devotion. It was thriving in the Charterhouse of Cologne when the storm clouds of the Reformation broke in the middle of the 16th century. It was here that St Peter Canisius heard of the devotion which he later passed on to his fellow Jesuits.

In the early 17th century, two Frenchmen, one in the North and the other in the East, made an important contribution to the devotion. St John Eudes promoted devotion to the hearts of both Jesus and Mary with great zeal in his native Normandy. In 1672, just before the visions at Paray-le-Monial, he celebrated a Mass of the Sacred Heart in his own order with ecclesiastical approval, something that would only happen in the Universal Church a century and a half later. St Francis de Sales, the Bishop of Geneva, was equally convinced of the value of this devotion.   He hoped that it would be a distinguishing mark of the spirituality in the Visitation, the Order he founded along with St Jane Frances de Chantal. It was fitting that one of its members, St Margaret Mary, should be the recipient of the most significant and far-reaching revelations in the whole history of the devotion.

THE GREAT REVELATION

One of the best known stained glass windows in Catholic churches features St. Margaret Mary kneeling before Jesus as he draws her attention to his Heart. She had only been a member of her community at Paray-le-Monial near Lyons for four years when the Risen Christ appeared to her around the Feast of Corpus Christi in 1673. Some years later in her autobiography, written under obedience, she described what happened, "showing me His Divine Heart, he said:' Behold this Heart which has so loved men that It has spared nothing, even to exhausting and consuming Itself to prove to them Its love. (cf Appendix B) In return, I receive from the greater number nothing but ingratitude, contempt, irreverence, sacrilege, and coldness in this Sacrament of my love. But what I feel still more is that there are hearts consecrated to me who use me thus. Therefore I ask of you that the Friday after the Octave of the Blessed Sacrament be kept as a special Festival in honour of my Heart, to make reparation for the indignities offered to It and as a Communion day, in order to atone for the unworthy treatment It has received when exposed upon the altars. **I also promise that my Heart shall shed in abundance the influence of Its divine love on all those who shall honour It or cause It to be so honoured"'**. This great revelation was the culmination of other revelations which had begun two years earlier and which were a cause of great distress and confusion to Margaret Mary. She thought she was having hallucinations. It

THE HEART OF JESUS: PURIFYING AND SANCTIFYING LOVE

The Heart of our Saviour is a burning furnace of love for us, of purifying, illuminating, sanctifying, transforming and deifying love.

His love is a purifying one in which hearts are purified more perfectly than gold in a furnace; an illuminating love which scatters the darkness of hell with which the earth is covered and admits us into the wonderful brilliance of heaven: He called us from darkness into his own wonderful light (1 Peter 2, 9); a sanctifying love which destroys sin in our souls in order to establish the kingdom of God there; a transforming love which makes doves out of serpents, lambs out of wolves, angels out of beasts, children of God out of children of the devil, children of grace and blessing out of children of wrath and malediction; a deifying love which makes gods of men, letting them share the holiness of God, in his mercy, his patience, his kindness, his love, his charity and his other divine perfections: sharing in the divine nature (2 Peter 1:4)

The Heart of Jesus is a furnace of love which spreads its fiery flames in all directions, in heaven, on earth, and throughout the whole universe. Its fiery flames would have consumed the hearts of the Seraphim and enkindled all the hearts of the earth if the terrible chill of sin had not set in. Jesus has an extraordinary love for men, the good as well as the wicked, for his friends as for his enemies, for whom he has such intense charity that even the overwhelming torrents and floods of their innumerable sins are not able to extinguish it: A love no flood can quench, no torrents drown (Song of Songs 8,7)

Oh sacred fires and flames of the Heart of my Saviour, rush in upon my heart and the hearts of all my brothers.

Imagine all the charity, all the affections, all the tender and intimate feelings of all the hearts that the omnipotent hand of God might fashion as being collected and united in one heart large enough to contain them. Would they not all be capable of forming one unimaginable furnace of love? Know, then, that all the fires and flames of such a furnace would not make one tiny spark of the immense love with which the loving Heart of Jesus is inflamed towards you.

Oh, who will grant me to be plunged into that burning fire? Oh Mother of Jesus, Oh all you Angels, Oh all you holy Saints of Jesus, I give myself to you and I give you all my brothers and sisters in Christ, all the inhabitants of the earth, that you may cast us all into the abyss of that sacred furnace!

St John Eudes (1601-1680)

was not until she met Claude la Colombière, who assured her that it truly was the Risen Christ who had appeared to her, that she was able to accept the authenticity of what was happening in her life.

It was the humility and obedience of Margaret Mary that most impressed Claude as he tried to assess the genuineness of her reported revelations. She had absolutely no pretensions to being a "visionary". In fact, she saw herself as totally inadequate to the task of spreading devotion to the Heart of Christ. But the Lord made it clear that it was precisely because of her limitations that He had chosen her. A person of very obvious natural talents would have been tempted to attribute to her own enterprise and energy the great things the Sacred Heart was about to bring about in the Church. It was also clear to Claude that she was a totally obedient religious who did not want a life in any way different to that of the other nuns in her convent. Her superiors accepted Claude's favourable judgement on her revelations but made sure that these extraordinary events were not common knowledge among the other nuns. In fact it was only after Claude's death and the publication of his diaries that the nuns at Paray-le-Monial put two and two together and concluded that Margaret Mary was the "chosen soul" he referred to. (cf. Appendix D)

On June 21st, 1675, the actual Friday after the Octave of Corpus Christi, these two future canonised saints consecrated themselves to the Sacred Heart and offered themselves to suffer all things for the realisation of His designs. This is the first instance in the Church of two people consecrating themselves simultaneously to Christ. Until then consecration was a term normally reserved to an act carried out by one person to the benefit of another. For instance, a king was consecrated by a bishop or a bishop was consecrated by another bishop. The joint consecration of Margaret Mary and Claude was asked for by the Lord himself and initiated a tradition that would have enormous influence on Catholic practice in succeeding centuries.

What these two friends in the Lord did on that day has inspired countless individuals, families, religious orders and indeed whole nations to consecrate themselves to the Sacred Heart. The Morning Offering, one of the most beloved and consoling practices of Catholic piety, has its origins in the act of the two saints, as has also the Pioneer Offering. But perhaps the most important of these acts took place more than two centuries later on June 11, 1899, the Sunday after the Feast of the Sacred Heart, when Leo XIII consecrated the universe to the Sacred Heart. He described this as the greatest act of his pontificate. And this from the man who gave us the epoch-making encyclical on the need for justice in the modern world - *Rerum Novarum!* It would be difficult to over estimate the good that would emanate from the joint efforts of these two chosen souls.

With the death of Claude la Colombière on February 15th, 1682, Margaret Mary lost her great friend and supporter.   In the eight years remaining to her until her own holy death on October 16th, 1690, she had to look for other helpers in carrying the Sacred Heart message of love to the whole world. As a contemplative nun she herself could not preach or promote it outside her own monastery. On divine inspiration she contacted a young Jesuit student, Jean Croiset, and told him that, once ordained, he was to carry on the work of his one-time spiritual director, Claude la Colombière. His most important commission would be to write a book with her help. She warned him that the work would bring him much trouble and suffering but also guaranteed that one day the Lord would richly reward him for his efforts.

Margaret Mary herself did what she could within the confines of her monastery. As Novice Mistress and with the approval of her superiors she introduced the devotion to the young women in her charge. This took the simple form of erecting a shrine around an image of the Sacred Heart painted by a Sister Joly to Margaret Mary's specifications and modelled on her vision. What prompted this was a promise the Lord had made to her, "I will bless every place in which an image of my Heart is exposed and honoured". Before long, this simple practice was proving its worth in the remarkable growth in holiness evident in the lives of the young nuns and it soon spread to other monasteries of the Visitation. By the time she herself was canonised in 1920, it had become the favourite icon and a source of spiritual strength in tens of millions of homes around the world.

Margaret Mary's dealings with Jean Croiset at the beginning were only by letter. For such a retiring silent person her letters, still extant, were untypically long and even wordy. It is touching to see how she herself is aware of this and wonders how Croiset will have the patience to read them to the end. She writes like someone "driven". He only knew her through these letters until a short time after his ordination she invited him to come and see her. He brought along a Jesuit friend. They were both dreadfully disappointed with their meeting. They found her so timid, inarticulate, indecisive and unimpressive that they decided not to accept her invitation to return to the monastery the following day. However, at breakfast next morning each of them felt an overwhelming urge to return and shared this with the other. When Margaret Mary came into the parlour this time, she seemed a different woman. Afterwards they said that it was as if they were in the presence of an empress who seemed to be towering over them and who was so authoritative that they felt like small children in her presence. They left her with a desire to spend their lives spreading the message she gave them. Croiset said afterwards that a possible explanation for her tongue-tied condition at the first visit was her upset that he had shared the matter of her letters with the other Jesuit.

Croiset had the book substantially written before Margaret Mary died and she said of it that it was so completely in accordance with the wishes of Our Lord that it would never be necessary to make any change in it. Given its subsequent history, there is much irony in this assertion. The first edition of the book which he entitled *Devotion to the Sacred Heart of Jesus* appeared in May 1691, seven months after Margaret Mary's death when Croiset had no qualms about revealing her identity and her extraordinary life. In fact he added an excellent biography of her at the end of the book. This has to be the most influential book ever written on devotion to the Sacred Heart. It has been instrumental in giving the devotion the shape that it has taken over the centuries and in leading eventually to the canonisation of Margaret Mary in 1920. In the thirteen years after it was published it went through numerous editions. This, however, did not bring much pleasure to Croiset. His Father Provincial of 1691 was enthusiastic about the book but this changed with his successor. He set up a commission of theologians to examine Croiset's teachings. They ruled against him and he lost his post as professor of theology and was sent away from Lyon lest he should be an influence in the lives of young Jesuits. Eventually this ruling was overturned. Through it all, Croiset remained totally obedient to his superiors and clung personally to his devotion to the Sacred Heart.

In 1704, the saga of the book took its strangest turn. It was placed on the Index of Forbidden Books. Apparently, not because of any doctrinal errors but because it did not conform to some bureaucratic formalities. This did not prevent some enterprising Italians from translating the original French into their own language. This Italian edition led to the spread of the devotion all over Europe. Yet this wonderful book remained officially on the Index for 183 years ! In 1887, Archbishop Stadler of Sarajevo wanted to consecrate his arch-diocese to the Sacred Heart and came across Croiset's book which he had translated into his own language. He was about to publish it when he was told that it was on the Index. Undaunted, he asked the Sacred Congregation to have a look at it and make whatever changes were necessary. They submitted it to the most searching examination in the light of Papal Encyclicals and Decrees of two centuries and found that there was no trace of error in it and that no change was necessary. Permission was given to translate it into all the languages of the world. And as St Margaret Mary had said, not a single iota in it had to be changed.

DEVELOPMENT AND DIFFICULTIES IN THE 18TH CENTURY

Jean Croiset was joined by another Jesuit, François Gallifet, in promoting and indeed defending the Devotion in the early decades of the 18th century. They both had to suffer for their exertions. Besides the banning of Croiset's book, Gallifet, an Assistant to the Superior General in Rome, was reprimanded by his superiors for being over zealous in promoting what was perceived as an untested novelty in Christian life. The Devotion met fierce resistance in Jansenistic circles where it was seen to concentrate so much on the mercy of God that it totally overlooked his justice. It was the mercy-filled promises revealed to Margaret Mary to which they objected most (cf Appendix F). But it also met resistance in the most orthodox quarters. Prosper Lambertini, Promoter of the Faith (later to be more favourable to the Devotion as Pope Benedict XIV), rejected Gallifet's pleas for a feast in honour of the Sacred Heart. He perceived a danger in Gallifet's assumption that the heart was the "seat of sentiment", an unproven philosophical position. However, the story took a new turn when Monsignor Languet, the Bishop of Soissons and an influential member of the Academie Française, agreed to champion the cause. In 1729 he published his monumental biography of Margaret Mary. It set in train the developments that led to the successful request to Rome by the Polish bishops in 1765 for a feast in honour of the Sacred Heart, as the Lord Himself desired, according to Margaret Mary. From then on, requests poured in for an extension of the Polish privilege to the whole world. As the saint herself had predicted, there would be no stopping this devotion, once the faithful heard about it.

While the theologians were arguing about the niceties of the devotion it was already making an impact on the lives of people. It was put to the test early in the 18th century when the plague broke out in Marseilles. A ship from North Africa docked there early in 1720 with at least two carriers of the bubonic plague on board. It spread like wildfire through the city. Out of a total population of about 90,000 upwards of 50,000 died. Sr. Anne-Madeleine Remuzat, a Visitation nun like Margaret Mary, had predicted this scourge and when it broke out, Our Lord himself showed her that the remedy lay in devotion to his Sacred Heart.

The Bishop of Marseilles, Henri de Belsunce, made a public Act of Reparation and Consecration of the city to the Sacred Heart with dramatic effect. Within hours the plague stopped. Two years later it broke out again. This time the City Council associated themselves with the Bishop in a solemn vow to the Sacred Heart. The plague ended dramatically again. Ever after Marseilles has considered itself the City of the Sacred Heart. The news of this happening in such a cosmopolitan place as Marseilles soon travelled to the ends of the earth.

As early as 1707 the word had reached China since a Father Romain Honderer dedicated a church to the Sacred Heart there in that year. There was a booklet on sale in Dublin and Waterford in the 1750's promoting the devotion and the Limerick-born poet, Tadgh Gaedhlach Ó Súilleabháin was a member of a confraternity in Dungarvan where the devotion was promoted. His poem "Gile mo chroí, do chroí-se, a Shlánathoir" (My heart's dearest love, O Saviour, is Your Heart) is certainly compatible with it. In Spain the great promoter in those days was Bernard de Hoyos, (1711-35), who died in the odour of sanctity and a professed Father of the Society of Jesus at the age of 24 (!). In December 1995 Pope John Paul 11 declared the heroicity of his virtues, an important step towards eventual canonisation. In 1733 when he was asked to translate the book of Fr Gallifet he was so impressed that he decided to devote the rest of what would turn out to be the two remaining years of his life to spreading the Devotion. He made that decision on May 3rd, 1733. Two days later the Lord showed him His Heart as he had done in the life of St Margaret Mary. His efforts produced extraordinary fruit in that short space of time as practically the whole Spanish

Hierarchy consulted him for advice and direction. The good effects of his work are still apparent in the widespread Sacred Heart devotion in the Spanish speaking world.

With the French Revolution, the devotion led to death for many of its adherents. A young woman, Victoire de Saint-Luc, used to make little cloth emblems of the Sacred Heart which people wore as a religious emblem. They were known as "sauvegardes". Some rabid revolutionaries chose to see these as anti-revolutionary symbols and Victoire and her parents were sentenced to death for producing them. She tried to defend herself by saying that she had been sending these things to her friends for years before the Revolution broke out. Her explanation was rejected and on 19th July,1794 she mounted the scaffold with her parents. The executioner was embarrassed at his involvement in such blatant injustice. Victoire took the initiative, walked first to the guillotine and said to her parents, "you showed me how to live, now I am going to show you how to die".

The Society of Jesus was suppressed in 1773 but not before it had taken up the cause of the Sacred Heart devotion and vigourously defended it against its Jansenist opponents. One of the last acts of Fr Ricci, the Superior General at the time of the suppression, was to consecrate the order to the Sacred Heart. It would not be restored for another forty years. With the collapse of civic order in France and the destruction of so much organised religion around Europe, triggered off by the Revolution, many of the faithful turned to the Sacred Heart in their distress. This sustained them through a long winter as they took comfort from the Psalmist's words about the heart of God. "His own designs shall stand forever, the plans of his heart from age to age" (Psalm 33,11). Happily, the next century would eventually reveal some of the wonderful things the Lord was preparing behind the unpromising appearances where a Pope was imprisoned, the eldest daughter of the Church in revolutionary turmoil and Europe in the thrall of the first modern dictator.

PHENOMENAL GROWTH IN THE 19TH CENTURY

The new century had scarcely begun when St Madeleine Sophie Barat, on November 21st, 1800 founded the Society of the Sacred Heart. It was the first fruits of a rich harvest that would increase all through the century and indeed continue into the next. What Madeleine Sophie did has been replicated by an impressive number of founders and foundresses ever since. Besides inspiring the foundation of these religious congregations, during the 19th century Sacred Heart devotion made its way into ordinary Church life with dramatic effect.

In the first half of the century, two popular movements in particular made an enormous contribution to this development; the setting aside of a whole month, June, as a time of special devotion to the Sacred Heart and the growth of the Apostleship of Prayer. Both these developments began in France. The first of them had its highly unlikely origins during the 1830s at Les Oiseaux, a girls' secondary school in Paris. Angèle de Sainte Croix, one of the boarders, was distressed because she could not get into the Children of Mary. She had too many "black marks" against her! Reverend Mother told her that a visit to the Blessed Sacrament and a prayer to the Sacred Heart would put everything right. In the course of her prayer she concluded that it was not fair that Our Lady had a whole month to herself and that the Sacred Heart had none! Reverend Mother suggested that she pass on this idea to the Archbishop of Paris during his next visit to the school which Angèle duly did. His Grace took up her proposal enthusiastically and decided on the spot to dedicate the month of June to the Sacred Heart for the conversion of sinners and the return of France to the Church. The idea spread around the world like wildfire. It is now an accepted part of Catholic life. The second of these movements dates from 1844 at a House of Studies at Vals in the South of the country where the young Jesuits were finding their studies long and tedious. They could not wait to get out into the mission fields. Fr Francis Xavier Gautrelet convinced them that the best thing they could do for the spread of the Kingdom, while they were students, was to offer up their efforts to the Sacred Heart in a spirit of prayer. In the light of this, he set himself two goals: "to spread the faith through prayer", by which he meant harnessing the energies of the Mystical Body for the spreading of the Gospel, and at the same time helping pious people to transcend their selfishness by getting them interested in the great problems of the Church, especially the missions, "through zeal and charity, which draw man out of himself". His idea caught on in other religious congregations. Another young Jesuit professor of philosophy at Vals, Fr Henri Ramière, saw the apostolic potential of spreading this idea to people in all walks of life and dedicated his life to promoting it. By the time he died in 1884, there were 35,000 centres of the Apostleship of Prayer, 13 million members and 14 magazines called "Messengers of the Sacred Heart" around the world. Fr Cullen, founder of both the Irish Messenger and the Pioneers, was profoundly influenced by the work of these two zealous French Jesuits.

The Lord had revealed to Margaret Mary His desire that a feast in honour of His Sacred Heart be established on the Friday within the Octave (eight days) of Corpus Christi. That was in 1675. In this matter, the mills of God ground very slowly, for 181 years to be precise. On August 23rd, 1856, the desire was fulfilled when Pius IX extended the feast, which had been conceded to certain groups, to the Universal Church. The rarity of this event can be appreciated when we realize that only two other new feasts in honour of Our Lord have been introduced into Catholic liturgy in the last thousand years: Corpus Christi in the 13th century and Christ the King in the 20th. The introduction of this new feast in the middle of the 19th century had the desired effect of an increased devotion to the Sacred Heart, still happily flourishing in the whole church.

The beatification of Margaret Mary herself in 1864 and her canonisation in 1920 placed the seal of approval on the apparitions at Paray-le -Monial and her own teaching. Her message was eventually "carved in stone" when the French people, under the leadership of President Marechal de Macmahon, constructed the Sacré - Coeur, the great Basilica at Montmartre, one of the best known landmarks in the world and dedicated it "To Christ and His Most Sacred Heart from a Penitent and Devout France". The Devotion reached a highpoint as the 19th century closed when Leo XIII consecrated the whole human race to the Sacred Heart on June 11th, 1899. He revealed his mind in *Annum Sacrum*, the encyclical on the Sacred Heart written a few weeks earlier on May 25th,1899:

"*When the Church, in the days immediately succeeding her institution, was oppressed beneath the yoke of the Caesars, a young emperor saw in the heavens a cross, which became at once the happy omen and cause of the glorious victory that soon followed. And now, today, behold another blessed and heavenly token is offered to our sight - the most Sacred Heart of Jesus, with a cross rising from it and shining forth with dazzling splendour amidst flames of love. In that Sacred Heart all our hopes should be placed, and from it the salvation of men is to be confidently sought.*"

DEVELOPMENTS IN THE 20TH CENTURY

Devotion to the Sacred Heart got off to a flying start in the twentieth century, much facilitated by Leo XIII's great act which had been inspired by a revelation to a German-born nun, Maria Droste in a Portuguese convent. Our Lord had made known to her his desire to have the human race consecrated to his Heart which she was to pass on to the Pope. His Holiness took the request seriously. She herself suffered terribly from an excruciatingly painful spinal disease towards the end of her short life and died on Thursday June 8, the eve of the Feast of the Sacred Heart. It was only three days afterwards on the Sunday following, June 11, that the Pope solemnly consecrated the universe to the Heart of Jesus. It was also in 1899 that the Litany of the Sacred Heart, one of our most beautiful prayers, was approved for use in the universal Church. (cf. page 59). Many churches all over the world were dedicated to the Sacred Heart and much public worship, such as widespread Holy Hours of Adoration, became rooted in the devotion.

One of the most significant developments in the devotion was the widespread practice of Enthronement of the Sacred Heart in homes. Fr Mateo Crawley-Boevey (1875-1960) a Peruvian priest of the Congregation of the Sacred Heart, was the indefatigable promoter of this good cause, in spite of bad health in the early part of his life. The son of an English convert and a Peruvian Catholic mother, he believed that Enthronement could "change the face of the earth". However, when he asked Pope St Pius X for permission to implement it, the Pope feigned refusual. But this was simply the prelude to something more wonderful. "No, my son...you ask permission, and I say, 'No.' Not only do I permit you, but I command you to give your life for this work of social salvation". On leaving the Pope he went straight to Paray-le-Monial where he experienced an extraordinary interior illumination as well as a restoration to perfect health. During this enlightening experience he came to understand that the devotion to the Sacred Heart, usually associated with churches and chapels, was now to be brought into the family circle. Until his death in 1960 even two World Wars could not put a stop to his extraordinary gallop, bringing happiness to millions of homes on the five continents.

CONTRIBUTION OF MODERN POPES

Pius XI, (1922-39) in his encyclical *Miserentissimus Redemptor* (May 9,1928) stressed the importance of reparation as an indispensable dimension of the devotion. Using the simple notion of the need to repair, whether what is broken is something material or a significant human relationship, His Holiness appealed to Christians to honestly face up to the "obligation which rests upon all of us to make those amends which we owe to the Most Sacred Heart of Jesus." During the Great Depression he wrote a second encyclical, *Caritate Christi Compulsi* (May 3, 1932), where he described devotion to the Sacred Heart as "the extraordinary remedy for the extraordinary needs of our times". There was no exaggeration in his phrase with the terrible massacres of the Spanish Civil War and the conflagration of World War 11 just around the corner.

In his very first encyclical Pius XII (1939-1958) spoke of his love for the Sacred Heart and announced that spreading devotion to the Divine Heart of Christ the King and Saviour was to be the beginning and end of his pontificate. In 1956, to mark the centenary of the extension of the Feast of the Sacred Heart to the whole church, he wrote *Haurietis Aquas,* one of the most important documents ever written on the devotion. In it he examined the foundations and values of the devotion and invited scholars to delve more deeply into the matter and begin a more thorough study of its riches.

In the personal diaries of John XXIII (1958 -1963), one of the most loved Popes of modern times, we get an idea of his intense love for the Heart of Jesus: "Every time I hear anyone speak of the Sacred Heart of Jesus or of the Blessed Sacrament, I feel an indescribable joy...These are loving appeals from Jesus who wants me wholeheartedly there at the source of all goodness, his Sacred Heart, throbbing mysteriously behind the Eucharistic veils. The devotion to the Heart of Jesus has grown with me all my life. I want to serve the Sacred Heart today and always. It is to the Heart of Jesus that I must look for a solution to all my troubles. I want the devotion to his Heart, concealed within the sacrament of love, to be the measure of all my spiritual progress. I am determined to give myself no peace until I can truly say I am absorbed into the Heart of Jesus." These precious words give us some insight into the mind and heart of the man who summoned the Second Vatican Council and became known as the Pope of Unity.

Popes Paul VI and John Paul II both reiterated in the strongest possible terms the teaching of their predecessors. Paul VI saw the Second Vatican Council as giving its total approval to the devotion as something relevant to our times when he wrote "Everyone sees that it is the most ardent wish of the Ecumenical

Council, by wise design and under the impulse of the Holy Spirit, to develop this (the devotion) in the hearts of the faithful."

Pope John Paul II reminded the Jesuits that the spread of the devotion was a mission entrusted to them by Christ himself (cf appendix E), to which they should dedicate themselves with renewed vigour: "I desire that you pursue with persevering action the spread of the genuine cult of the Heart of Christ, and that you may be always ready to lend effective help to my brothers in the episcopate in order to promote this cult everywhere, taking care to find means most appropriate to present it and put it into practice, so that the people of today, with their mentality and their sensitivity, may find in it the true response to their questions and expectations."

CONCLUSION

Ever since the Beloved Disciple saw the blood and water flow from the pierced side of Jesus on Calvary countless believers have been looking in spirit "on the one whom they have pierced". They may not have always thought in terms of devotion to the Sacred Heart but this was the substance of what they were doing. They felt themselves called, as St Anselm of Canterbury would put it, to pass through the opening in the side right into the wounded Heart Itself. Pius XII was alluding to this when he said "only those have a proper understanding of Jesus Christ crucified who have penetrated the mystic secrets of his Heart". St Margaret Mary was in this line of great lovers of the Heart of Christ: Bernard of Clairvaux, Bonaventure, Catherine of Siena and Teresa of Avila. Inspired by the Lord she did all in her power to pass on this message of love to the whole world. On one occasion when the Lord appeared to her, He was accompanied by his Blessed Mother who did all the speaking. (for a fuller account of this event cf Appendix E). She wanted Margaret Mary and all her Visitation sisters "not only to enrich themselves with this treasure but to do all they can to put this precious money in circulation. They must distribute it lavishly, trying to enrich the whole world with it without fear of depleting it". With the help of her Jesuit spiritual director, Saint Claude, Margaret Mary did make this great treasure available to the whole world. She was not inventing something new. She was simply drawing attention to the immense treasure of love in His Heart.

Until her death at 43 years of age, Margaret Mary exhausted herself in finding ways to make this message known. She began by consecrating herself to the Sacred Heart and then encouraging others to do the same. She wrote to priests and seminarians asking them to preach about it. One simple thing she did was to circulate pictures of the Sacred Heart painted by one of the other sisters in the convent. This was in response to Our Lord's promise "I will bless the homes in which the image of my Sacred Heart is exposed and honoured". The wearing of the Pioneer pin is inspired by this promise. Fr Cullen reasoned that if the Lord was prepared to be so generous to those who displayed the image of His Heart in the privacy of their homes, what would he not do for those who wore it publicly on their person. Even modern advertising has seen the potential of linking the image of the heart to love. Margaret Mary was way ahead of her time! It is because of her initiative, that millions of people around the world begin each day with a simple offering of themselves to the Sacred Heart (see the formula on page 65). They also consecrate their homes to the Sacred Heart (see page 66-68) and experience the effects of another of the consoling promises, she revealed. "I will give peace in their homes". From personal experience they can corroborate the assertion of Pope Pius XII: " It is impossible to exaggerate the excellence of devotion to the Sacred Heart. If we consider the external practice of the devotion, we must admit that it is a most perfect way of professing the Christian religion. It is indeed no more nor less than the religion of Jesus".

Fr Pedro Arrupe, one time Superior General of the Society of Jesus:

If you want my advice, I would say to you, after 54 years of living in the Society and almost 16 of being its General, that there is a tremendous power latent in this devotion to the Heart of Christ. Each of us should discover it for himself- if he has not already done so- and then, entering deeply into it, apply it to his personal life in whatever way the Lord may suggest and grant. There is here an extraordinary grace that God offers us.

From a letter addressed to all Jesuits on February 6, 1981

Chapter Two

Reflections on the Heroic Offering

O Sacred Heart of Jesus
For Thy sake to give good example
To practise self-denial
To make reparation to Thee for the sins of intemperance
and for the conversion of excessive drinkers
I will abstain for life from all intoxicating drink
Amen.

The Pioneer ideals are encapsulated in the above short offering prayer which members recite twice daily. Fr Cullen, the founder, first proposed it during a Temperance Mission in St Peter's Church, Falls Road, Belfast on St Patrick's Day, 1889. Later, in conversation with a fellow priest, he explained how he came to formulate the offering, which he was prepared to describe as "heroic". He asked himself what were the highest reasons for which a person could do anything in this world. He eventually concluded that there were no higher ideals in life than the glory of God and the salvation of both ourselves and others. After much prayer and reflection, he incorporated these ideals into an easily memorised formula, rooted in ordinary human experience. This simple prayer has featured in the personal devotion of hundreds of thousands of people ever since. The late Fr Harris of the Diocese of Kildare and Leighlin, who died in Naas, Co Kildare in 1978, provided us with this information. His own parish priest earlier in the century had been the confidant of Fr Cullen.

Fr Daniel Dargan S.J., Central Director of the Association, 1953-77 shares the following reflections on the Heroic Offering and other aspects of Pioneer life.

FOR THY GREATER GLORY
Fr Cullen made his own the motto of St Ignatius of Loyola, founder of the Society of Jesus to which he belonged, *Ad maiorem dei gloriam* (for the greater glory of God) and made it the basis of the Association. The expression is reminiscent of the words of the early Father of the Church, St Irenaeus,

"Gloria enim Dei vivens homo, vita autem hominum visio Dei" (the glory of God is the person fully alive but true life for the person is the vision of God), *Against the Heresies IV, 20, 7*. Fr Cullen saw the Association as contributing to a fuller life for individuals and families and wanted to ensure that no one would fail to reach the vision of God through abuse of alcohol.

AND CONSOLATION

The notion of consoling the Suffering Saviour has motivated the great Christian mystics through the ages and was very much part of the religious culture in which Fr Cullen was reared. It was seen as an effort to respond to the invitation implied in such texts as: "Insult has broken my heart past cure. I hoped for sympathy, but in vain, for consolers - not one to be found" Psalm 68(69),20 or the plea to Peter in the Garden of Gethsemani "Could you not watch one hour with me?" Matt. 26: 40. In a world where so much of public and private life is the very antithesis of the clearest expressions of the mind of the Saviour, this aspect of Pioneer spirituality still has a profound relevance.

FOR THY SAKE

People who abstain from alcohol may have various reasons for doing so, such as health, saving money or fear of becoming an alcoholic. We make use of such reasons in so far as they help us but from the beginning, Fr Cullen emphasised that love for the Sacred Heart was to be the outstanding motive for Pioneers, and after a hundred years, the driving force behind all our work, efforts and promotion is love for the Heart of Jesus.

Pioneers should therefore try to deepen their devotion to the Heart of Jesus. To best understand the Heart of Jesus, we should look at the Christ who walks through the Gospel pages, the Christ who loves us.

TO GIVE GOOD EXAMPLE

In today's world many are put under pressure to drink alcohol and are made to feel the "odd man out" when they resist. This is particularly unfair to anyone who has a drink problem and knows that total abstinence is a must for him/her. Young people, unsure of themselves and anxious not to be regarded as "different", may be laughed at because they do not take alcohol. Often they are told that "everybody drinks". This incidentally is untrue. A recent survey taken in Ireland showed that one third of the adult population were abstainers. Nevertheless it is hard for young people to stand up to such pressure, and the temptation to give in can be strong. Many young people who have broken their pledge have said afterwards that they did so because they succumbed to pressure to do something they didn't really want to do.

One valuable service of a Pioneer is to make the point that people's right to drink what they want should be respected. If one person has the right to take alcohol then another has an equal right to take a non-alcoholic beverage or indeed no beverage at all.

The presence of an abstainer in the company can be a source of strength to someone who does not really want to take alcohol. Often Pioneers are quite unaware that their example has been a big help and support to others.

Example by parents, be it for good or otherwise, is a very big influence in the life of their children. Many parents are influenced by this motive in becoming Pioneers. They want to do their very best knowing that children are more impressed by what parents do than what they say.

TO PRACTISE SELF-DENIAL

The present wave of permissiveness and self-indulgence is doing incalculable harm to our society. This is seen in the extent of family break-up, drug and alcohol addiction, violence, sexual abuse, corruption and the business scandals constantly being brought to our notice.

All of this spotlights the importance of self-control, self-discipline, self-denial, and makes clear that a society without these qualities is heading for disaster. Selfish living and self-indulgence drag down; it is self-sacrifice that builds up and achieves what is worthwhile.

Self-sacrifice is an essential part of Christian life. It challenges us in imitation of Jesus Christ to take up the cross, follow Him and share in His sufferings. "If anyone will come after me let him take up his cross and follow me". Self sacrifice leads to the personal freedom that carrying the cross brings. 'Anyone who loses his life for my sake will find it' Matt. 16:15. The Pioneer Association is rooted in a spirit of self-sacrifice. (cf. Appendix D)

Freedom from excess or addiction enables us to live life to the full. By making themselves free and independent of alcohol pioneers will find themselves able to put their talents, energies and time (which some waste by immoderate drinking) to better use, a better service of God, neighbour and country.

"Be very careful" says St Paul, "about the sort of life you lead, like intelligent and not like senseless people. Do not drug yourselves with wine. This is simply dissipation". Eph. 5:15,18.

TO MAKE REPARATION

A mother was left a widow with four young children to bring up. In her great love for her children, no sacrifice was too great for her when she felt she could do something for their welfare. The children grew up, married and left home. The three eldest however began to lose interest in their mother, ignored her, neglected her. The youngest, a child, seeing this, went out of her way to make up to her mother, and made many sacrifices in her desire to make up for the bad treatment the other members meted out to their mother. This is reparation, a notion familiar to us all.

Reparation to the Sacred Heart of Jesus means making up to Him who loves us so much, making up for the sinful ingratitude shown to him not only by other people, but also by ourselves. It is not enough for us to look at the questionable behaviour of others, we must be concerned about our own.

Christ said: "As long as you did it to one of these the least of my brethren you did it to me". His words afford us a practical way of making reparation. We can offer words of support, acts of kindness to help to make up to people who have been rejected, hurt, snubbed. Countless opportunities of making reparation are given to us in this way.

There are many other ways in which we can make up to Him. We do so especially by giving Him a loving and faithful service and also by acts of self-sacrifice, a readiness to put ourselves out for the sake of others. Fidelity to our lifelong promise with the difficulties that this may involve, is an obvious way in which Pioneers make up to Him. And finally, willing acceptance of the daily crosses that come to us in life is a genuine form of reparation.

FOR THE CONVERSION OF EXCESSIVE DRINKERS

After years of excessive drinking a man went to Alcoholics Anonymous and gradually succeeded in overcoming his problem. Telling his story to a group of Pioneers he said: 'it took me a long time to admit that I was unable to give up drinking by simply wanting to. At last, after repeated falls I came to accept that I just couldn't control my drinking of my own accord. That was the day when I really turned to God, and admitted my powerlessness and asked his help. And that was the first step for me on the road back. It has been a tough struggle. I thank God that I am sober today. We in AA know that you Pioneers offer your pledge and prayers for people like us and we value what you are doing.'

In his mercy God has arranged that we can help one another by our prayers and sacrifices. We offer our pledge and prayers to win from God grace and help for the one who is trying to overcome a habit of heavy drinking.

Christ has spoken of a devil cast out by prayer and fasting. The devil of intemperance can be cast out by prayer and fasting from alcohol. Many people join the Pioneer Association with the intention of taking part in a crusade of prayer for a relative or friend whose drinking has gone out of control.

In our prayers we should make sure to remember also the family of the intemperate drinker. For them life can be hard. They often have to suffer humiliation, unhappiness in the home and doing without things they would normally expect to have. Indeed the fortitude of so many relatives of irresponsible drinkers is quite heroic.

WHY THE NAME PIONEER?

One difficulty that faced Fr James Cullen was to decide what name should be given to the new Association. Finally, he hit on the name Pioneer. It was an excellent choice; Pioneer is an exciting name and a challenging one. A pioneer is not a conservative stick-in-the-mud. Rather, he is a leader, one who goes forward, who is to the fore in promoting sobriety. A Pioneer should be a person of initiative, courage and enthusiasm.

The early Pioneers won widespread support because they were seen to be filling a need. They were showing the community that something effective could be done to counter drinking excesses, that people could lead worthwhile lives without alcohol. At that time many people had become dejected, feeling that nothing could be done to lessen the widespread intemperance around them. The new Pioneers brought hope.

As Pioneers we should be humbly grateful for what our membership has done for us and for countless others. It is indeed a very significant value in our life, a value we should not lock away from others, but be eager to pass it on in a society where it can do so much good.

If he had difficulty in arriving at the title Pioneer, Fr Cullen had no doubt as to who should be the patron of the Association. He himself had a deep personal love for and trust in the Sacred Heart. He founded the Irish Messenger of the Sacred Heart, and spent much of his life promoting the devotion. It was only natural then that he would name the Pioneer Association after the Sacred Heart.

PIONEER PIN - A SYMBOL OF LOVE

As Pioneers we are trying to follow in the steps of Jesus Christ. If He was anything, he was a man of caring and compassion. His heart went out to the sick and suffering, the have-nots and oppressed, the handicapped and the victims of discrimination. They were told that they were nobodies, with no one to support them. They were even told that God had no time for them, that they were sinners. Jesus, however, told them that God loved them dearly and was very close to them. He showed them kindness and understanding and lifted up their hearts. He freed them from their illnesses and gave them a sense of their human dignity. Our Pioneer emblem reminds us that we are here to proclaim the love of Christ, to bring His love to a world often cold, hard and selfish. In the light of this, I see a Pioneer as a person of caring Christian love, ready to give unselfish service, to bring hope and encouragement.

Thankfully, it has always been the tradition of the Association that our members give help and support to those who need it. They do this by being kind to an invalid or disabled person, by assisting an elderly neighbour, by caring for the sick or bereaved, by listening with understanding to the troubled and heavily burdened.

Many Pioneers, as members of charitable organisations, willingly give generous help to others. Many Pioneer groups organise events for the benefit of the blind, the sick, the poor, the victims of alcoholism. This is only right. It would be strange to reduce ourselves to a group that prays, but has no practical concern for the problems, needs, difficulties of others, no awareness of opportunities for action. A love for Jesus that does not find expression in love for people, is not the charity of Christ and is sadly lacking.

THE COMPASSIONATE JESUS

Anyone reading the Gospels cannot but notice how His love goes out especially to those in suffering and in pain. Whoever is afflicted has a priority claim on Him. Constantly the Gospel tells us how He was moved to compassion at the suffering of others. A leper, sick and rejected, appeals to Him, knowing that in Jesus he has a real friend. And Jesus responds warmly. Deeply touched by the man's plight, He not only speaks to him with sympathy and kindness, but He stretches out His hand, touches him and says: "Be thou made clean". And the man is instantly restored to full health. (Mk. 1:40)

THE FORGIVING JESUS

Jesus was known as the friend of sinners, and perhaps this is the title that, above all, makes us want to draw close to Him. After all, we are all sinners. In the Gospel, we see how wrongdoers, the wayward, sense His forgiving love and go to him with hope - so much so that the Pharisees openly disapprove of Him.

But if His readiness to mix with those who have broken God's commandments brings down severe criticism on Himself, He pays no heed to that criticism. On the contrary, all the more openly He asserts the right of such people to His love. "They that are in health need not a physician, but they that are ill. I am come to call, not the just, but sinners to repentance."

We see His great delicacy of feeling in dealing with people. How He stands up for the woman taken in sin and how He saves her from being stoned to death. "Has no one condemned you? Neither will I condemn you. Go now and sin no more."

On Good Friday, even as He hangs on the cross in agony, He has a word of forgiveness for the penitent thief: ``This day you will be with me in paradise." There is the Sacred Heart - ever ready to forgive.

A MOTIVATING FORCE FOR LIFE

I like to think of a Pioneer as one who, in trying to respond to the love of Jesus Christ, commits himself to the following of Christ. The love of the Heart of Jesus has become a motivating force in his life. Not that a Pioneer is in any way immune from sin. Far from it. But he is trying to draw nearer to Jesus. The words of a modern musical - words which 450 years ago were a favourite prayer of St Ignatius - indicate his goal: Help me to know you more clearly, love you more dearly, follow you more nearly.

The Pioneer who grasps this sees at once that his abstinence is not the be-all and end-all, it is only part of a commitment to Christ. A Pioneer should have high Christian ideals and strive to live up to them. It would, therefore, be totally inconsistent for a Pioneer to be practising abstinence and yet deliberately indulging in seriously sinful practices. Such behaviour, in addition to being very wrong, also draws the name of the Association into disrepute. In our founder's mind, Pioneers were to be not merely non-drinkers, but rather people committed to Christ, with a positive programme of prayer, self-sacrifice and example. Our abstinence was not to be of a selfish nature but to spring from a concern for others.

THE LORD LOVES A CHEERFUL GIVER!

We know that the majority of people drink alcohol. We accept this as normal and therefore it is not for us to be critical of them. Still less should we grudge them their drink. We must never foster a 'sour grapes' mentality: I don't drink, so I don't like to see you drinking either. Drinking in moderation is good and reasonable, and if no one drank to excess, people would enjoy a much better quality of life. Having made our commitment we should be serene and content in this. God loves a cheerful giver as Scripture tells us, and the Catholic tradition is to make a sacrifice with a smile. But we must be realistic and recognise that excessive drinking is wrong, and to be rejected. Anti-drink the Pioneer Association is not, anti-drink abuse we certainly are.

If we Pioneers make a sacrifice, this should not lead us to be gloomy or morose. Rather we should be cheerful people, glad to be able to do something for the Sacred Heart, conscious that compared with all that He has done for us, ours is indeed a small sacrifice.

Chapter Three

Talks on Temperance

The Pioneer dies to drink that others might live
Fr Sean McCarron S.J. (1907-1975)

The excerpts given here are from talks given at Pioneer meetings through the years. The speakers have all remained faithful to the original charism of Fr Cullen. He believed that alcohol was a divine gift. But pastoral experience convinced him that without the further gifts of wisdom and self control it would be abused. He encouraged prayer and self-denial as means for spreading sobriety within the Mystical Body of Christ. This chapter begins, appropriately, with the full text of a talk given by Fr Cullen himself to an immense audience in the City Hall, Cork, in 1911 when the Association he founded was already an established institution in Irish life and he himself the most experienced and successful temperance promoter since Fr Mathew. It must rank as the most authoritative ever given on the subject.

THE PIONEER MOVEMENT. ITS STORY AND ORIGIN

My dear Pioneer friends - it would be difficult for me to exaggerate the pleasure which it gives me to meet you tonight, or to express my gratitude adequately, for the invitation you have given me to address this great Temperance demonstration. I need hardly add that this privilege is greatly increased by the interest which, in common with you, I attach to the public expression of the people of Cork on this question, so vitally important to the Irish nation. And I take it that few amongst us will not recognise that a meeting of such proportions as this is all the more pressing at this present juncture of our history, when we stand at the parting of the ways; and after centuries of struggle we are allowed to begin to shape, according to our own views, the destiny of our country.

Largely on the solution of the problem which we are here to-night to discuss will, I believe, depend the future of Ireland, for, if Ireland be sober Ireland shall be free, but if Ireland elects at this eventful stage of her history still to hug the chains which so long have fettered her freedom, and still refuse to employ the unimpeded use of the splendid facilities with which Providence has so liberally endowed her children, then, in vain shall we possess the blessings of Home Rule, in vain shall we have our own Parliament in College Green, in vain shall the flag of Erin float over a people, degraded and demoralised by intemperance. I think I do not err when I say that a large and growing section of the Irish people are convinced that the future of our nation will be mainly determined by the attitude which the country now takes on this momentous question, involving, as it unquestionably does, its life or its death knell. Speaking for myself, it was not to-day or yesterday that I arrived at this unalterable conviction, for it has been the growth of many years of observation and experience. While still a young priest, now more than forty years ago, I saw that the curse, as well as the ruin, of Ireland was strong drink.

The cause which had led up to the woeful habit of confirmed national intemperance, I was not able then clearly to determine, for Irish history, viewed from a social standpoint, was scarcely known in those sad, far-off days. Our enemies generally affirmed that such vices were of our own making, while natural virtue we had to learn from the victorious stranger. True, people who thought more kindly of us, considered our intemperance was largely due to the dampness of our Northern climate, or to the sad necessity of drowning the despair of a weaker nation crushed by a stronger one which had, doubtlessly, plundered her of her liberty, her lands, her language and her parliament. We remember that it was also tried, but, thank God, unsuccessfully, to stamp out her religion, as may be seen still even in our day in the alienated or ruined churches, the dismantled shrines and monasteries of Ireland. Other social economists regarded this Irish drink habit as the inevitable outcome of our Celtic character. "We were a drinking, fighting, happy-go-lucky people," they said. "A lovable, sociable, good-natured, intelligent people, admirably fitted to be the servants or slaves of the Saxon conqueror, admirably suited to live in, but not to own, the fair island that gave us birth." Whatever may have been the explanation of our drinking customs, this sad picture of a Nation's folly was shrouded in still deeper gloom at the time by the fact that a few years previously one that seemed raised up by Providence to be a saviour to his country had appeared, and the radiance of his advent was, as of a sun in the East, filling the sky with light and making the heart of Ireland throb, as it had not throbbed for centuries, with new life and hope! That saviour of his country was Fr. Mathew, and his adopted home was Cork.

There is no need, in this his own city, to dwell on his marvellous history or recount his triumphs. Under the magic influence of his personality, Ireland, like another Samson, rose in her might, burst her drink bonds, and led by Daniel O'Connell, began to breathe again the breath of liberty. But alas! this radiant vision was all too bright to last. The glory of Tabor was to be succeeded by the night of Calvary! And so, in Ireland, to the triumphs of Fr. Mathew's apostolate succeeded the black famine years of '46 and '47, leaving hundred of thousands to die by the roadsides of the fruitful land of which they had been plundered. The crowbar brigade and the emigrant ship so fully completed the awful work of Erin's devastation that in the darkest night of Erin's sorrow only some faint notes of her muffled harp told of a nation's agony. All this terrible tragedy I had dimly recognised in these by-gone days of forty years ago, but, thank God, even then I never wavered in the hope that brighter days would come for Ireland, and that the pendulum which had so long and so sadly swung backwards, would, when God's own hour had struck, once more swing forward to herald hope and prosperity for Ireland.

In addition I felt that the glorious example of Fr. Mathew was too precious an inheritance for a young Irish priest to lose sight of, and that, however feeble or inadequate he might be, still he might try at least to tread in the footstep of the great temperance leader and continue his work for that land and that race which Father Mathew had loved, and so practically laboured for down to his latest breath.

Inspired by thoughts such as these, I ventured from the very outset of my priesthood to grapple with the vice of intemperance, but I quickly found that my struggle was a deadly one with a modern Goliath, and undertaken by me, who was a poor substitute for David, as I possessed neither his skill, nor his sling, nor the fatal stone with which he slew the giant Philistine. Fortunately for me at this time, while still a priest on the secular mission in the Co. Wexford, I had for my Bishop one to whom Ireland will be ever deeply indebted for the resuscitation and marvellous assistance which he gave to the temperance cause; I allude to the Most Rev. Dr. Furlong, then Bishop of Ferns.

It was this remarkable Prelate who first began to administer the Total Abstinence Pledge to children at their Confirmation who, unaided by civil law, established Sunday and Holy Day closing of public houses throughout his whole diocese, and transferred public fairs and markets from Holy Days to week days. Everybody knows that this beneficent legislation still flourishes in the County Wexford and bears abundant fruit in the visible comfort and prosperity of its people. And here, I will crave your indulgence to allow me, passingly, to advert to the very conspicuous part which the County Wexford has long sustained in the temperance campaign. In New Ross, a town in that county, in the year 1829, ten years before the advent of Fr. Mathew, the Rev. George Carr, a Protestant clergyman, started a temperance pledge movement against the use of alcohol; many years afterwards we have seen what splendid work Dr. Furlong achieved in the temperance movement. Bishop Warren, his saintly successor, himself an ardent temperance advocate, publicly took the Total Abstinence Pledge in the pulpit of his own Cathedral in Enniscorthy, and thus initiated and carried on a most successful Total Abstinence Crusade, which has left a deep and lasting impress on the whole diocese of Ferns. The Anti-Treating League, which has so powerfully helped to eradicate the silly and deplorable habit of "treating", was founded by Father Rossiter, Superior of the Missionaries in Enniscorthy, while Father Columbus Maher and, still later, Father Nicholas Murphy, both distinguished Capuchin Fathers and both closely identified with the glorious Capuchin temperance work in Church

Street, Dublin, are descendants of the men of '98. But to return to my story, from which these old and cherished memories of Wexford made me digress. For some years I toiled beside Bishop Furlong and Bishop Warren in this great conflict, but the experience of these years convinced me that no large measure of success could be achieved by the methods we had followed. True, an enormous work had been done; one county, at least, in Ireland, had been thoroughly wakened from the torpor of drink, and the foundations of a great edifice of social reform had been laid.

On every side the pledge was taken by thousands, but on the other hand the pledge-breaking was considerable, and to me it was most disheartening.

FATHER CULLEN TAKES THE PLEDGE

And so I was led to venture on a new experiment. On Rosary Sunday, 1874, after the celebration of Mass in the little country chapel of Glynn, in the County Wexford, where I was then engaged on a Mission, it struck me that without Fr. Mathew's example of absolute total abstinence, by way of example and sacrifice for others, the larger success I hoped for could not be attained. Although previously, through my life, I had taken but little stimulants of any kind, I resolved, for the sake of good example, to give up even that little. From that morning I have never wavered in my allegiance to that cause, and, though loss of health, death itself, and a premature grave as the consequence of cold water drinking were ominously predicted by crowds of friends, I am living still, thank God, a fair old specimen of the beneficial results of total abstinence from all alcoholic drinks. *(He lived to 80 years of age).*

Years went on under the new auspices, and still I felt that the outcome of the efforts made by my priestly companions and myself was not commensurate with our work. On the whole to me it was unsatisfactory and disappointing. Some further developments should be tried, and the development came in this wise. Some time after I had joined the Society of Jesus I was engaged in a temperance retreat in Belfast at the request of Bishop McAlister. The customary "spiritual exercises" were performed. Each night St. Peter's vast church was packed to overflowing, and the usual Total Abstinence Pledge was to be administered on the last Sunday to the immense crowd. Such scenes I had frequently witnessed and shared in before. The enthusiasm, the fervour, the apparent resolution to keep the pledge faithfully, the deep roar of voices pronouncing the solemn words of the pledge were all well known and long familiar to me. But the subsequent and alas! the too frequent violation of that undertaking, so frequently demonstrated by experience, stared me in the face, and I struck!

I would not any more ask the pledge to be recited aloud and taken indiscriminately by all. Only to those, henceforth, should I administer it, who, on calm reflection, were prepared to make the life sacrifice to total abstinence and give me their names and addresses! Naturally, this view met with opposition on all sides, the procedure was an unbidden innovation, the life engagement was made too drastic, the trial was doomed to failure, for it was believed that the crowds, shrinking from the "hard word," would go away no better for the Temperance Mission.

FIRST HEROIC OFFERING

However, I was inexorable, and would not yield. On the last Sunday night of the mission in the pulpit of St. Peter's, Belfast, I announced the conditions of the new pledge which I styled the "Heroic Offering". Contrary to all expectation, about three hundred adults, the very cream of the congregation, came up to the altar rails and subscribed their names to the new Temperance venture. Thus we started the "Heroic Offering" in the capital of the Black North!

Again some years passed, and still I was not satisfied with the progress of temperance. The thought grew on me apace that what, above all, was needed, as a striking feature of a successful total abstinence crusade, should be the example of sacrifice given to the weaker brethren by those who had no need of the "Heroic Offering" for themselves. This sacrifice should be unselfishly and cheerfully made for others.

PIONEER ASSOCIATION FOUNDED

To work out this idea, on the 28th December 1898, I invited four ladies to meet me in our Presbytery, Gardiner Street, Dublin. These ladies were already veteran and uncompromising total abstainers. Mrs. A.M. Sullivan was the leader of our tiny band. The others were: Mrs. Bury, Mrs. Egan and Miss Power. At our little round table conference I informed them briefly of my previous disappointments, and unfolded the new project and my hopes for its success. Was it only to be another dream to be followed by another disillusionment? God alone knew this, but we all hoped at least for the contrary. I then told them that during many years I had endeavoured to begin temperance work at the footrung of the ladder, by administering the total abstinence pledge to all who sought it, and with results which, though moderately successful, were by no means what I had anticipated. Henceforth, with their aid, I said I would begin at the top rung of the ladder and gradually coming down, would stretch a saving hand to those who needed it below. In other words, into this Pioneer Association, only those on whose example of life perseverance we could thoroughly rely would be admitted. Only those could be members who had never taken a strong drink at all or had taken it in strict moderation, or who, by long probation, had proved their stability in the practice of total abstinence. The name of the new Association would be the "Pioneer Total Abstinence League of the Sacred Heart". It would be composed of two grades - namely, Pioneers and Probationers. Both sections should take the life pledge against all intoxicants. All Pioneers, without exception, should have completed two full years of rigid total abstinence, while probationers were those who were passing through these two years of waiting. Pioneers should be sixteen years of age; probationers could be admitted at fourteen. The Juvenile Total Abstinence

Association of the Sacred Heart for children under fourteen was also started.

To counteract the tyranny of human respect, to bring our members out into the open, to make them know one another whenever they met, to inspire the courage and comradeship which springs from the sympathy of members, we determined that all our members should openly wear a distinctive emblem of their undertaking. It would be a pin, pendant or brooch of the Sacred Heart, always publicly worn as an outward visible sign of membership, and as a token by which we might all recognise ourselves as soldiers fighting until death for a noble cause and under the standard of the Heart of Jesus.

Only after a searching investigation, often antecedently, could members be admitted as Pioneers or Probationers by Pioneer Councils established at each "Centre" of the work. In the year 1905 our Holy Father, Pius X,. sent his blessing to the Pioneer enterprise and enriched it with copious indulgences.

TO BEGIN WITH WOMEN

At the beginning of the work, I may state that I intended to admit none but women to our Pioneer membership. I began in this way, because I knew that women have ever been by word and example the world's greatest social reformers. I knew also that the world, viewed from the moral standpoint, is in a great part, for good or for evil, what the women make of it. No word is truer than that. "The hand that rocks the cradle rules the world" and so every woman, directly or indirectly, be she wife, mother, daughter or helper, shares in this mysterious privilege and power. Of this fact I was fully convinced despite all countervailing arguments. Moreover, I felt that, as a rule, women deserved exceptional sympathy, because they were the greatest sufferers in the wreckage caused by drink - they were but too often the hidden, silent, uncomplaining victims of its cruelty and of its savagery. It was this insatiable, selfish monster of drink which robbed themselves and their little ones of housing, food, clothes, education, religion and extinguished every prospect of betterment in their lives. It was drink which condemned them to hunger, loathsome rags and squalor, until a merciful death came to put an end to their lives of hopeless misery. In fighting for temperance they would be fighting, as no other could fight, for themselves and for their children, for earth and for heaven.

CORK

This eventful meeting of the first four Pioneers took place in December 1898, and immediately preceded my starting for a second time on missionary enterprise in South Africa. I hoped that during my twelve months of absence that the first battalion of the little Pioneer army, entirely composed of women, would pave the way for future conquest. The women leading the way, I believed that the boys and men, in due course, would surely follow. However, before embarking for this distant missionary undertaking I was one of a number of Jesuits detailed for a mission in the Church of Saints Peter and Paul, here in your own city. In one of the sermons I explained the origin, scope and conditions of the new movement, and asked for the assistance of some brave women in Cork to give it a helping hand. That night there was a hearty response to the appeal. Perhaps a dozen or more, qualified for instant admission, gave in their names, and the work was begun.

FIRST MEN PIONEERS

But on that same night a strange occurrence took place which materially altered the whole plan of my campaign. On leaving the pulpit and reaching the sacristy I was confronted by a number of earnest young men, who complained that they were not allowed to assist in the good cause. I replied that on my return from Africa I had resolved to begin recruiting amongst men for the next battalion of Pioneers. But one, who seemed to be the spokesman of the others retorted: "But, Father, if you should never come back, perhaps we should never have a chance of becoming Pioneers at all!"

His reasoning was irresistibly conclusive. I gave way and answered: "Well, in God's name we will start the men's battalion to-night here in Cork"! And so in the old sacristy of Saints Peter and Paul's Church was begun the second great wing of the Pioneer army. And thus, too, it fell out that the "Heroic Offering" originated in Belfast, developed into the Pioneer movement in Dublin, and finally was crowned in Cork!

Fr Cullen lived for a further ten years, dying in Dublin on December 6th 1921, the same day as the signing in London of the fateful Anglo-Irish Treaty.

AN HONOURABLE AND SACRED COMBAT

His Holiness Pope Pius XI spoke on the question of abstinence from alcohol to a group of Catholic Total Abstainers of the League of the German Cross on September 30th, 1930. The message would have been equally appropriate to a group of Pioneers.

"You are especially welcome because you represent a society and an endeavour which we praise very particularly.

Your endeavour is not only a good work, it is an honourable and sacred combat, a beneficent fight, a combat for God and for the individual. Continue your beautiful work, continue your combat with courage, with increasing courage and with great determination. The fruits of your battle will not be wanting; they are incomparable fruits, a source of happiness in the first place for you and your families.

The Church rejoices in a very particular way over your activity because you co-operate in a distinguished manner in an apostolate, in a genuine apostolate to which she is committed; you have chosen a way which will enable you to save many souls and also many bodies."

Pope Pius XI, 1930

From Revue Antialcoolique des Cercles Lacordaire et des Cercles Ste-Jeanne d'Arc. Boston, Mass, Octobre-Novembre- Decembre, 1930,pp.231-232.

PIONEER ASSOCIATION - INSPIRED BY GOD

I firmly believe that in founding the Pioneer Association, Father Cullen was inspired by God in basing the whole movement on the realisation of the insult offered to God and the destruction wrought in the soul by the sin of the drunkard. And I need hardly refer to what I am sure you are all thinking of - that inspiration came to him in your own city of Belfast, for it was here that he first wrote down the words of the "Heroic Offering." This was the inspiration that has kept the Pioneer movement upon the straight path. I want to emphasise this point, because there are men, even good and sincere Catholics, who call us extremists, who think that the Pioneers, of all the people in the world, are not keeping straight. Well, if an extremist in the matter is one who realises to the full the awful insult offered to God by sin, the awful devastation it works in the human soul and who is prepared to make any sacrifice to atone to God for that sin, or ward off that devastation, then we are Pioneers and proud of it.

Fr Fergal McGrath SJ, speaking in 1931 in Belfast.

I GIVE IT TEN YEARS

"How long do you think the Pioneer Association will last," was a question put to me twenty years ago by a priest- who then prophetically answered his own question: "I give it ten years." My reply was: "The Pioneer Association will last as long as it is left on the lines laid down by Fr Cullen."

When Fr Cullen was nearing his end, he had one fear, one dread. It was, that those who would come after him in charge of the Association would start changing the rules and methods." If they do," he said to me more than once, "they will ruin it." The Association as it stands is the result of fifty years of failure and success. Each restriction was shown to be necessary by previous failures. Rule after rule was planned to check what experience had shown to be causes of lapses in the past, and to bar excuses that had made pledge breaking easy.

Scarcely was he dead when assaults were made on me that had been broken time and time again on his iron will. It is interesting to note that with the solitary exception of one rule, every suggestion of change was in the direction of making the rules easier. They said: "The rules were too strict... unreasonable... but we ought to allow this drink or that other...that there are circumstances when we should allow a drop or several drops...and that the doctor rule is too hard...that poor people could not get the doctor, etc." You know it all. I stood firm. Further I said to myself: Father Cullen was fifty years at the work. His experience was tremendous. I shall, therefore, be a long time in charge before I dare to set my judgement against his.

Twenty years have passed. I have changed nothing, and am proud that to-day the Pioneer Association is the Pioneer Association which Father Cullen left.

Fr Joseph Flinn S.J., immediate successor of Fr Cullen,
Theatre Royal, Dublin 1942.

NO SMALL SACRIFICE

That there is self-denial and often great self-denial needed to be faithful to the Pioneer pledge is beyond all doubt. For we forgo, not just the pleasures of appetite in the moderate use of drink, but we forego, too, all the social value of a drink–the companionship it brings, the spirit of comradeship, the sense of friendly intimacy. All this we sacrifice. We are prepared, too, to face the embarrassment which human respect will cause when our refusal to drink is wilfully misunderstood, or taken as a slight: we are prepared to suffer the sting of sarcastic bitterness which labels our resolution as pious hypocrisy.

Freely and deliberately we choose to bear all these, that the little it costs us may be effective for the saving of others.

Fr Sean McCarron S.J., Central Director, Theatre Royal, Dublin, 1942

DRUNKENESS CAN BE CURED

"Drunkenness can be cured. Every year witnesses conversions from excessive drinking. Of course God listens to and answers prayers, provided that these prayers are earnest and persevering. For his own wise reasons, God may defer the giving of special graces to the drunkard for a long time and thereby, amongst other results, develop in those who continue to pray a deep spirit of faith and trust, detachment from the good things in life, zeal for souls and many other magnificent virtues."

Fr Paddy Doherty, S.J., Assistant Central Director, Irish Catholic, 28/1/54

NO DRINK, NO ENJOYMENT?

The notion of merriment, in the minds of many, is invariably linked with the notion of drink. No drink, no enjoyment, they believe, while they look on the life of a teetotaller as a state of continuous boredom. A glance through the reports of excursions and socials organised by Pioneer Centres and confined to members of the Association, shows that these ideas are false.

Fr Paddy Doherty, S.J., ibid. 8/9/55

AN INDISPENSABLY NECESSARY DYKE

Dearly beloved sons and daughters, children of Catholic Ireland, who could be more welcome in the home of Christ's Vicar ?

Your presence always brings joy and consolation, because an Irish pilgrimage at once reminds one of the high and holy mission given by Providence to an entire nation, an eminently apostolic mission with the whole world for the exercise of its zeal, and one bows before the inscrutable wisdom of God directing the fulfilment of that mission.

It shines out so luminously from the pages that tell the story of Ireland's faith.

'Who will separate us from the love of Christ ?' was the vibrant challenge of St Paul. 'Will affliction or distress or persecution or hunger or nakedness or peril or the sword ?...Yet in all this we are conquerors through Him who loved us.' (Rom. 8, 35).

May not St Patrick, speaking for his children, echo the Apostle of the Gentiles? Like a rock amid the waves, relentlessly turning over the ages, the Faith of Ireland with her filial loyalty to the See of Peter, has remained unshaken.

Oh, never forget the glory of the past. Thus may its brightness still shine on the hills and lowlands, the countryside and the cities of your people. But it is not of this that we would speak to you today.

Let us rather open Our paternal heart and share with you very briefly one or two anxious thoughts.

The first is suggested by the Association represented by practically all of you here present.

Proverbially Ireland is a land that combines the smile and the tear. And alas, what a flood of tears, drowning out the joy and laughter of home and hearth, has poured through the shattered dyke of temperance.

Your Pioneer Abstinence Association of the Sacred Heart is a valiant attempt, fortified by a genuinely Pauline spirit of self-denial for the spiritual advantage and need of one's neighbours, to repair and strengthen that indispensably necessary dyke, and we have only words of praise for your generous charity.

Our anxiety indeed goes beyond Ireland. In more than one country of the world, intemperance in drink, leading so often to alcoholism, has become to-day a harrowing menace and an actual spiritual tragedy for thousands of souls redeemed by the Passion and Death of Jesus Christ.

Who will number the homes broken by this sin? Who will weigh the amount of good for souls left undone because of this sin ?

It is a social evil and a spiritual deterioration that calls for the enlightened study and self-sacrificing zeal of every apostle, lay and cleric.

With heavy heart We contemplate the extensive area of blighted hopes, and with grateful affection We bless those who, by word and especially example, set themselves to remove the cause of the evil.

Then We cannot help feeling some anxiety when we reflect on the continued emigration of so many of your people from the land of their fathers. Will their Faith continue to be their guiding and protecting star ? Will it still be the priceless inheritance received so, We might say, casually from those who stood ready to give their life in its defence.

To them the thought never occurred that their religion could have a price. Will the Faith that flourished in the sheltered garden at home still thrive in an atmosphere that may be chilling and frosty?

A comfortable materialism too easily takes possession of a man in the hard hour of misfortune, and stealthily may come to filch from him what deep down in his heart he knows is his highest and best good.

Your devoted and beloved Bishops are alert to the danger and their guidance will afford protection to those who must leave, while the special need of the immigrant will be another sharp spur to the apostolic ambitions of Our dear and worthy sons, God's priests busy in the vineyard of the Lord.

And now to you, beloved sons and daughters of Catholic Ireland, We impart the Apostolic Benediction, and We extend it to all your loved dear ones at home. May it be a pledge of God's richest blessings on you and on your dear Ireland.

Pope Pius XII, 1956

Address delivered to a Pilgrimage of Pioneer members of the Garda Siochana (the Irish Police Force).

BEING "THE ODD MAN OUT"

"Let no one under-estimate the magnitude of the sacrifice you have made. It is a big sacrifice and it is a continuing sacrifice. You have given up something which you know is not evil in itself, you have made a sacrifice which you need not have made. That sacrifice you began when you made your Heroic Offering; that sacrifice you renew every day; that sacrifice hurts every time you feel the desire to take a drink, when you are in company where others are drinking, when you don't want to be the "odd man out" and when, nevertheless, you strengthen your will and refrain. These sacrifices are hidden from men's eyes-but very often it is the hidden sacrifices which are the hardest; certainly it costs something and certainly, when it is inspired by a proper motive, it can be an act of pure love of Christ."

Most Rev.Dr William Conway, Bishop of Neve, later Cardinal Archbishop of Armagh and Primate of All Ireland speaking at the great Rally in Croke Park, June 14th, 1959

COMPASSIONATE AWARENESS

"Among the Irish pilgrims we warmly welcome members of the Pioneer Total Abstinence Association of the Sacred Heart. On the occasion of your Seventy-fifth Anniversary we exhort you to continue in your praiseworthy efforts to help eliminate the disorder of alcoholic abuse from society. This is done by prayer and the sacrifice of abstinence which you gladly offer to God in reparation for the misuse made of his good gifts. This is likewise furthered by a compassionate awareness of the complex physical, psychological, moral and religious aspects of the disorder itself. We earnestly hope and pray that the joyful sobriety of your own lives and the Christian love and service which you show to all whose lives are affected by this grave problem may indeed serve to strengthen the moral fibre of society and bring closer to it the healing and sustaining hand of Christ the Saviour.

Pope Paul VI, 1974

This truly inspired summary of the role of the Pioneer in society was given at the Papal audience on October 9th during the 75th anniversary pilgrimage to Rome.

WE WILL NOT PASS BY ON THE OTHER SIDE

God could not have blessed the Pioneer Association so abundantly had it not been authentically Christian. The three-fold marks of genuine religion always have been and always will be prayer, fasting and alms-giving. Our Association will continue to receive the blessings of the Lord to the extent that it is characterised by all three: to the extent that we give ourselves to both the spiritual and corporal works of mercy and compassion. With the example before us of Jesus Himself, the Great Good Samaritan, we will not pass by on the other side of the road of life. He came to the help of suffering humanity with arms uplifted in prayer in Gethsemane, outstretched in suffering on

Calvary and extended in healing on the streets of Capernaum. Prayer without fasting and alms-giving could become so heavenly that it would be no earthly use. Fasting without prayer and alms-giving may be no more significant than dieting. Alms-giving without prayer and fasting indicates a desire to do good and avoid God.

Fr Bernard J. McGuckian S.J., Knock Shrine, 1979,
on occasion of the 80th anniversary of the Association

EXCESSIVE DRINKING ALARMED FRANK DUFF

"Frank Duff wore a Pioneer Pin. He did so as much to identify himself as a committed Catholic as to show concern for temperance. But excessive drinking alarmed him. It affected so many people, either as drinkers themselves or as sufferers through others' drinking and it was so difficult to break the habit. He studied the subject as closely as he could and passed on what he learned. Being a Pioneer at least helped by way of prevention, and nibbled away at alcoholism itself. The problem was painfully close to him. It affected his family to some extent and his visitation as a Vincentian brought him up against it on all sides.."

León Ó Broín on the Servant of God, Frank Duff,
Founder of the Legion of Mary.

THE ROBUSTNESS OF THE SUPERNATURAL

Natural problems cannot always be solved or alleviated by natural means. They need the robustness of the supernatural. They need the additive, the impregnation, the leaven of God's grace. The Pioneer recognises in a special way the spiritual dimension of the drink problem. In pursuit of a solution, he makes a sacrifice. As parents give up freedom; as celibates give up marriage; as Christ gave up life, the Pioneer gives up drink. Since Christ is hurt by all sin, including sins of intemperance, there is always need for reparation. Love of Christ will always be a supremely valid motive even if devotion to the Sacred Heart needs to be renewed and modernised. Since alcoholics are frequently helpless and their relatives invariably miserable, they need and will always need the support, the solidarity, the spiritual sustenance of the Pioneer's sacrifice and prayer. There is nothing negative or puritanical about the Pioneer's attitude to drink. There is something very positive and supportive about his attitude to Christ's people. Only when prayer and sacrifice become unnecessary will the Pioneers become irrelevant and these things will always be necessary because they are the ingredients of love.

Dr Joseph Cassidy, Bishop of Clonfert, later Archbishop of Tuam, speaking at
Knock Shrine, June 1982

THEY ARE SIMPLY AGAINST ABUSE

The Pioneers are a Catholic temperance movement. Their aim is to provide some solution to the problems created by the abuse of drink but their intention is to do this in accordance with Catholic tradition and spirituality. The best of Catholic tradition rejects puritanism. Puritanism would say, 'Drink is Evil'. Catholics cannot say that of anything God has made, and neither can Pioneers. The Pioneers are unusual among temperance movements in that they are not an anti-drink crusade. They are not against the use of drink generally. They are simply against its abuse, and above all against what its abuse can do to people, members of the body of Christ. Their aim is not to wage war on drink. They are a spiritual association, and for them the crux of the matter is not alcohol, nor even alcoholism, but sin. Their concern is people in difficulties, and their approach is a spiritual and caring one, by personal prayer and self-denial to help their fellow-members of the body of Christ who are in difficulties in this regard. The principle on which they work is that taught by St Paul in 1 Corinthians 12 (to be re-read over and over again) and expressed by Pope Paul VI as follows: 'By the hidden and loving mystery of God's design men are joined together in the bonds of a supernatural solidarity, so much so that the sin of one harms the others, just as the holiness of one benefits the others' (The Rite of Penance)

The methods of this association are the traditional ones recommended in the gospel, namely 'prayer and fasting' (Mark 9:29). In its support of fasting the Catholic tradition clearly does not imply that food and drink are evil. Similarly the Church praises celibacy for the Kingdom of God, but it holds that marriage is a sacrament. Pioneers support total abstinence, but they gladly acknowledge that wine goes into forming our greatest sacrament. As for all Catholics, so too for Pioneers, the Eucharist is central, but in their general approach to this sacrament the Eucharistic Cup has a particular significance for Pioneers in that it underlines the goodness of what they surrender by their undertaking in this association.

Fr Raymond Moloney S.J. Eucharistic Congress, Nairobi, Kenya, August 1985

IT IS BASED ON LOVE

The first and fundamental principle of the Pioneer movement is that it is based on love; not on fear; not on reasons of human prudence; but simply on love. The heart of our movement is the heart of Christ himself, and that heart is a heart of love. For us the beginning and the end can only be one fact, one truth, and that truth is love - Christ's love for the Father, Christ's love for us, our love for him and for the Father, our love for one another. Love is the motive. Love is the end. Love is the means. The heart of Christ to lead us and fill us and inspire us; that is what our movement is all about.

Fr William J. Reynolds S.J., Central Director,
International Pioneer Seminar, Dublin, 1986

QUALITY RATHER THAN NUMBERS

Fr Cullen deliberately set his standards for membership high and he was uncompromising in his demands for fidelity to those standards. He was more concerned about the quality of the commitment than he was about the large numbers of members. He expected nothing less than heroism from Pioneers.

Let there be no misunderstanding, however. Pioneers do not set themselves up as a spiritual elite or think of themselves as heroic persons. They simply see themselves as freely choosing a certain form of self-denial as one of their ways of "taking up their cross everyday" and following Jesus Christ. Devotion to the Sacred Heart, particularly under the aspect of reparation to the Sacred Heart for the pain caused to the heart of Christ by sins of intemperance, were and are an integral part of the spirituality of the movement and the main source of its motivation. It is not primarily by human means, however admirable in themselves, that the Pioneer Association hopes to counter the evil of drink abuse, but rather, through the "folly of the Cross of Christ".

Dr Cahal B. Daly, Bishop of Down and Connor, later Cardinal Archbishop of Armagh and Primate of All Ireland, on June 18th,1989 at Knock Shrine on the occasion of the centenary of the Heroic Offering.

SECULARLY RELEVANT AND SPIRITUALLY MEANINGFUL

"20 years ago a new theme at international meetings of sociologists of religion was the 'crisis of religion'. Today it is the 'crisis of secularisation'. The emerging 'autonomy of the secular' is not necessarily a bad thing... It is when it intrudes on the 'autonomy of the spiritual' that it reduces the quality and meaning of life for people. The Pioneer Association may be ideally placed to provide an essential service that is secularly relevant and spiritually meaningful. In theological jargon, the PTAA is 'incarnational' in character... The spirituality of the Pioneer Association will have to be re-examined in the light of contemporary culture. It has always been a fruitful Ignatian principle that we must always begin with the people where they are at the present time. Symbols and practices which no longer make sense to people must be changed. In my opinion, there is need to carry out some spiritual training or formation of Pioneers.

Fr Micheál MacGréil, S.J. from The Pioneer of the Future, paper read to an International Seminar, Wexford, March 1993

ADVERTISING PRESSURE

In present day Ireland, I believe that the greatest culprit in overbalancing (this) lever of reason in the context of drink is the agency of advertising and of drink sponsorship. Those who have vested interests put forward an inane plea. They say that advertising does not cause more people to buy more drink. A simple question. Why then do drink firms spend money on advertising? Is it altruism? The cold reality is that hard-headed business people spend hundreds of thousands of pounds only because they have coldly calculated that they will reap immeasurably more and that at whatever costs to the bodily, mental or spiritual health of their customers. Every trick and every psychological subtlety that a well- paid agency can think up as a bait is being used to lure the young and the unsuspecting. A repeating ploy which many of you have seen on television commercials on drink is to feature an attractive woman in the centre frame of the final shot and always close up to the advertised drink. Incidentally, why have feminists never made a protest about this abuse of their sex? Or is this, forsooth, to be regarded as an advance in the pseudo liberation? So much power is vested in advertisers that when anyone tries to expose the reality he is most likely to be painted as an extremist. And more insidious still, commercial interests have such a power grip on many of our media today that they can insist on having their known critics removed and banned from the airways. I speak from long personal experience.

What hope have we to reverse this trend? My confident hope is that our schools would include in their curriculum a major study of communication media to provide our youth with information and standards of critical judgement. At present we are releasing school leavers year after year into the polluted lake of this culture and we have never tried to immunise them with a wholesome education. A start is being planned. There is hope.

Fr Leon Ó Morcháin, August 1993 at Knock Shrine.

Chapter Four

Heartfelt Prayer

You have nothing to fear either for or from the person who prays
St. Augustine

Fr Cullen saw the Pioneer Association as primarily a prayer movement. Intense prayer was the secret of his own apostolic effectiveness. He revealed this on one occasion when he said, "for every one word I say to a sinner, if I am to do that sinner any good, I must say one hundred words to God". The prayers in this chapter have been left us by men and women known for their love of the Heart of Christ. They can help deepen our own prayer life. Prayer has to be continual . (cf. Luke 18,1).

MORNING PRAYER OF SALUTATION
TO THE SACRED HEART

I praise, bless, glorify and salute the most sweet and bountiful Heart of Jesus Christ, my ever faithful lover. I thank You for the constant care with which You protected me last night and offered to God the Father on my behalf, praise, gratitude and all the duties I owe him. And now, O my Lover of Lovers, I offer to You my heart, to be as it were, a rose in bloom, attracting Your eyes all day with its beauty and delighting Your divine heart with its fragrance. I offer it to You also as a chalice from which You may drink Your own sweetness, with all that You will graciously operate in my soul this day. More, I offer it to You as a fruit for Your banquet of most exquisite savour which eating, You will so take to Yourself, that it will feel blissfully conscious of being within You. I pray that every thought, every word, every deed, every stir of my will may be directed in accordance with the good pleasure of Your most generous will.

Blessed Mechtild of Hackeborn (1240-1298)

PRAYER FOR SELF-FORGETFULNESS

Sacred Heart of Jesus, teach me perfect forgetfulness of self, since this is the only way to find entrance into you. As all I shall do belongs to you, grant that nothing I do be unworthy of you. Teach me what I must do to come to the purity of your love in fulfilment of the desire you, yourself, have inspired in me. I have a great desire to please you but an even greater inability to do so without the special light and help which I can only hope for from you.

Lord, do your will in me. I am well aware that I oppose it, even though I wish not to. It is yours to do, Divine Heart of Jesus Christ. To you alone the glory of my sanctification, if indeed I do become holy- this is as clear as day to me. But it would be a great glory for you, and this is the only reason I wish to perfect myself.

Saint Claude la Colombière, S.J. (1641-1682)

ACT OF CONFIDENCE IN GOD

My God, I am so convinced that you keep watch over those who hope in you, and that we can want for nothing when we look for all from you, that I am resolved in the future to live free from every care, and to turn all my anxieties over to you. ' In peace I lie down and at once fall asleep, for it is you and none other, Lord, who make me rest secure' (Ps 4:8)

Men may deprive me of possessions and of honour; sickness may strip me of strength and the means of serving you; I may even lose your grace by sin; but I shall never lose my hope. I shall keep it till the last moment of my life, and at that moment all the demons in hell shall strive to tear it from me in vain. 'In peace I lie down and at once fall asleep.'

Others may look for happiness from their wealth or their talents; others may rest on the innocence of their life, or the severity of their penance, or the amount of their alms, or the fervour of their prayers. As for me, Lord, all my confidence is my confidence itself. This confidence has never deceived anyone. It is you and none other, Lord, who make me rest sercure. No one, no one has hoped in the Lord and has been confounded.

I am sure, therefore, that I shall be eternally happy since I firmly hope to be, and because it is from you, O God, that I hope for it. 'In you, Lord, I have taken refuge, let me never be put to shame' (Ps 31:1). I know, alas! I know only too well, that I am weak and unstable; I know what temptation can do against the strongest virtue; I have seen the stars of heaven fall, and the pillars of the firmament; but that cannot frighten me. So long as I continue to hope, I shall be sheltered from all misfortune; and I am sure of hoping always, since I hope for this unwavering hopefulness.

Finally, I am sure that I cannot hope too much in you, and that I cannot receive less than I have hoped for from you. So I hope that you will hold me safe on the steepest slopes, that you will sustain me against the most furious assaults, and that you will make my weakness triumph over my most fearful enemies. I hope that you will love me always, and that I too shall love you without ceasing. To carry my hope once for all as far as it can go, I hope from you to possess you, O my Creator, in time and in eternity. Amen.

Saint Claude la Colombière:

From a sermon preached at St James Palace in London while he was chaplain to the Duchess of York, Mary of Modena.

ACT OF CONFIDENCE IN THE SACRED HEART

Sacred Heart of Jesus, I come to you throwing myself into the arms of your tender mercy. You are my secure refuge, my unfailing and only hope. You have a remedy for all my ills, relief for all my miseries, reparation for all my faults. You can supply for what is wanting in me, in order to obtain fully the graces I ask for myself and for others. You are for me, and for all, the inexhaustible source of light, of strength, of peace, of perseverance and consolation. I am certain that my importunity can never weary you, certain too, that you will never cease to aid, to protect and to love me because your love for me, O Divine Heart, is infinite.

Have mercy on me, then, O Heart of Jesus, and on all whom I recommend to you, according to your mercy, and do with us, for us, and in us whatever you will, for we abandon ourselves to you with a full, entire confidence and conviction that you never abandon us either in time or eternity.

Sweet Heart of Jesus I implore, the grace to love you daily more and more.

Saint Madeleine Sophie Barat, 1779-1865

PRAYER OF TOTAL CONFIDENCE IN GOD

Father I abandon myself into your hands.
Do with me whatever You wish.
And for whatever You should do with me
I thank You.
I am ready for anything,
I will accept whatever You ask.

I desire nothing, Lord
but that Your will be done
both in me and in all your creatures.

Into your hands I commend my spirit.
I give myself to You, my God,
with all the love of my heart,
because I love you,
and this love drives me to give myself,

to abandon myself completely,
and with total confidence,
into Your hands,
for You are my father.

Charles de Foucauld, (1858 - 1916)

This holy Frenchman is featured among the great lovers of the Sacred Heart depicted in the mosaic in the Chapel of the Apparition at Paray-le-monial. Following his conversion, after leading a dissolute life as a young man, he lived as a hermit in the Sahara where he died violently at the hands of nomads.

A PRAYER OF VENERABLE MATT TALBOT (1856-1925)

I adore You, O most sweet Saviour, expiring on the Cross for our sake; I have not words to express my gratitude to You for the infinite goodness You have evinced in dying to redeem me. O Eternal Father! I offer You Your dear Son who hung on the tree of the Cross naked, torn, pierced with thorns and with nails, bleeding, languishing, suffering, expiring. Yes my God it is Your own and only begotten Son that I offer to You in this lamentable condition; receive His Divine Sacrifice, accept this offering that I make to You, it is my ransom, it is the blood of God; it is the death of God; it is God Himself that I offer You now for the payment and acquittal of my debts.

I offer Him also for the relief of the Souls in Purgatory - for the sick, the poor and the afflicted, the grace of a happy death, for the agonizing, the conversion of sinners, the perseverance of the just, and to impetrate for myself and for those especially dear to me the grace of dying in Your friendship and love as also the grant of their special urgent petition.

May the most just, holy and adorable will of God be ever accomplished in all things ; may it be praised for ever and ever. Amen

Our Father, Hail Mary and Gloria.

This prayer was one of the favourite prayers of Venerable Matt Talbot. A copy of it was sent to the Pioneer Association in 1996 by Miss Kathleen Carmody, who had been given some relics of Matt in 1939 by his sister, Mrs Susan Fylan. She acquired other relics later from his niece, Mrs Byrne.

PRAYER FOR THE GIFT OF THANKFULNESS

It is right to give him thanks and praise
always and everywhere.
Teach me, Lord, to live this prayer
that I may thank you every day
for everything.

I do at times give thanks for what seems good,
for health, success
for love and gain

for all that pleases self.
And yet how thoughtless, blind
to thank you not for what
is truly good:
for pain, unkindness, censure, blame,
for every hurt that comes from person, place or work.
By these keen instruments wouldst
Our Divine Physician
remove the harmful growths of self
to give new life;
Your own true Life
and peace abundantly.

But I am blind,
see not Your loving hand
then in resisting suffer more;
spoil Your work.
Had I accepted all with gratitude,
I might have long since been a saint,
and happy,
A grateful heart cannot be otherwise.

Forgive then, Lord, my blindness
and my squandered life
and give me light, this day, to see
Your chastening hand in all my hurts (nor blame Your instruments)
The grace to take each purifying cross,
And then give thanks with all my heart.

Anonymous

LITANY OF THE SACRED HEART

Lord, have mercy	Lord, have mercy
Christ, have mercy	Christ, have mercy
Lord, have mercy	Lord, have mercy

(Each Invocation is based on the adjoining scripture reference)

God our Father in heaven	have mercy on us
God the Son, Redeemer of the World	have mercy on us
God the Holy Spirit	have mercy on us
Holy Trinity, one God	have mercy on us

Heart of Jesus, Son of the Eternal Father	have mercy on us (Mt 16,16)
Heart of Jesus, formed by the Holy Spirit in the womb of the Virgin Mother	have mercy on us (Mt 1,20)

Heart of Jesus, one with the eternal Word
have mercy on us(Jn 1,14;Col 2,9)

Heart of Jesus, infinite in Majesty
have mercy on us (Mt 25,31)

Heart of Jesus, Holy Temple of God
have mercy on us (Jn 2,21)

Heart of Jesus, tabernacle of the Most High
have mercy on us (Heb 9,12)

Heart of Jesus, house of God and
gate of heaven
have mercy on us (Gen28;17 Jn1.51)

Heart of Jesus, aflame with love for us
have mercy on us (Lk 12,49; Eph 2,4)

Heart of Jesus, source of justice and love
have mercy on us (Heb 1,9)

Heart of Jesus, full of goodness and love
have mercy on us (Lk 18,19;Tt 3,4)

Heart of Jesus, well-spring of all virtue
have mercy on us (Ap22,1;Ph 4,7-9)

Heart of Jesus, worthy of all praise
have mercy on us (Ap 5,12-14)

Heart of Jesus, King and centre of all hearts
have mercy on us (Heb 2,8)

Heart of Jesus, treasure-house of wisdom
and knowledge
have mercy on us (Col 2,3)

Heart of Jesus, in whom there dwells
the fullness of God
have mercy on us (Col 2,9)

Heart of Jesus, in whom the Father is
well pleased
have mercy on us (Mt 17,5)

Heart of Jesus, from whose fullness we
have all received
have mercy on us (Jn 1,16)

Heart of Jesus, desire of the eternal hills
have mercy on us (Gen 49,26; Jn12,22)

Heart of Jesus, patient and full of mercy
have mercy on us (2 Thes, 3,5)

Heart of Jesus, generous to all who turn
to you
have mercy on us (Rom 10,12)

Heart of Jesus, fountain of life and holiness
have mercy on us (Is 12,3; John 7,37)

Heart of Jesus,atonement for our sins
have mercy on us (I Jn 2,2)

Heart of Jesus, ovewhelmed with insults
have mercy on us(Lam. 3,30)

Heart of Jesus, broken for our sins
have mercy on us(Is 53,5)

Heart of Jesus, obedient even unto death
have mercy on us (Ph.2,8)

Heart of Jesus, pierced by a lance
have mercy on us (Is 53; Jn 19,34)

Heart of Jesus, source of all consolation
have mercy on us (2 Cor 1,3)

Heart of Jesus,our life and our resurrection
Have mercy on us (Jn 11,25; 14,6)

Heart of Jesus, our peace and reconciliation
Have mercy on us (Eph 2,16-17; Col 1,20)

Heart of Jesus, victim for our sins	have mercy on us (I Jn 2,2; Heb 2, 14)
Heart of Jesus, salvation of all who trust in you	have mercy on us (Acts 4, 12; Heb 9, 28)
Heart of Jesus, hope of all who die in you	have mercy on us (I Thess. 4,15; Tt 3.7)
Heart of Jesus, delight of all the saints	have mercy on us (Ap. 19,7)

Lamb of God, you take away the sins of the world have mercy on us
Lamb of God, you take away the sins of the world have mercy on us
Lamb of God, you take away the sins of the world have mercy on us

V. Jesus, gentle and humble of heart
R. Touch our hearts and make them like your own.

Father, we rejoice in the gifts of love
we have received from the heart of Jesus your Son.
Open our hearts to share his life
and continue to bless us with his love.
We ask this in the name of Jesus the Lord. Amen

—This litany was approved by Pope Leo XIII (1810-1903) on April 2, 1899.

PRAYING WITH THE SCRIPTURES

Each day of his life Fr Cullen spent an hour in meditation according to a method of prayer handed on by St Ignatius in his Spiritual Exercises. By looking in faith on the Jesus of the Scriptures, Fr Cullen believed that the words of St Paul would become a reality in his life. "Let that mind be in you which was in Christ Jesus", Philippians 2,5. There is no better way to get to know and understand the Heart of Christ than to spend time with him in this way. This has been the experience of all the great saints (cf Appendix C). The following scripture passages can help nourish our faith.

NEW TESTAMENT PASSAGES

THE HEART OF JESUS CHRIST

The soldiers came and broke the legs of the first man who had been crucified with him and then of the other. When they came to Jesus, they found he was already dead, and so instead of breaking his legs one of the soldiers pierced his side with a lance; and immediately there came out blood and water.
John 19:31-36

CURE OF A LEPER

And a leper came to him beseeching him and kneeling, said to him. " If you will, you can make me clean." Moved with pity, he stretched out his hand and touched him, and said to him "I will; be clean". And immediately the leprosy left him, and he was made clean. Mark 1, 40-42

THE BEATITUDES

Seeing the crowds, he went up the mountain, and when he sat down his disciples came to him. And he opened his mouth and taught them, saying:
Blessed are the poor in spirit, for theirs is the kingdom of heaven.
Blessed are the gentle, they shall have the earth as inheritance.
Blessed are those who mourn, for they shall be comforted.
Blessed are those who hunger and thirst for righteousness, for they shall be satisfied.
Blessed are the merciful, for they shall obtain mercy.
Blessed are the pure in heart, for they shall see God.
Blessed are the peacemakers, for they shall be called sons of God.
Blessed are those who are persecuted for righteousness sake, for theirs is the kingdom of heaven.   Matt 5:1-10

PRAYER AND FASTING

Jesus rebuked the unclean spirit, saying to it " You dumb and deaf spirit, I command you, come out of him (the boy), and never enter him again". And after crying out and convulsing him terribly it came out and the boy was like a corpse; so the most of them said, "He is dead". But Jesus took him by the hand and lifted him up, and he arose. And when he had entered the house, his disciples asked him privately. " Why could we not cast it out ? And he said to them "This kind cannot be cast out by anything but prayer and fasting".
Mark 9;25-29

COME TO ME

Come to me all you who labour and are overburdened and I will give you rest. Shoulder my yoke and learn from me, for I am gentle and humble of heart, and you will find rest for your souls. Yes, my yoke is easy and my burden light.
Matt 11;28-29

THE GOOD SHEPHERD

I am the good shepherd; I know mine and mine know me.....and I lay down my life for my sheep. John 10: 14-15

A NEW COMMANDMENT

A new commandment I give you, that you love one another; even as I have loved you so you also love one another. By this will all know that you are my disciples if you have love for one another. John 13: 34-35

JESUS FASTS

Then Jesus was led by the spirit into the wilderness to be tempted by the devil. And he fasted forty days and forty nights and afterwards he was hungry. Mark 4:1-2

THE BREAD OF LIFE

I am the living bread which has come down from heaven. Anyone who eats this bread will live forever. John 6:51

CHRIST REFUSES WINE AT CALVARY

And they brought him to the place called Golgotha (which means the place of a skull) and they offered him wine mingled with myrrh, but he did not take it. Mark 15:22-23

THE RISEN CHRIST

Now I (Peter) and those with me, can witness to everything he did throughout the countryside of Judea and in Jerusalem itself; and also to the fact that they killed him by hanging him on a tree, yet three days afterwards God raised him to life and allowed him to be seen, not by all the people but only by certain witnesses God had chosen beforehand. Now we are those witnesses - we have eaten and drunk with him after the resurrection from the dead. Acts of Apostles 10:39-41

YOU ARE GOD'S CHOSEN

You are God's chosen race, his saints; he loves you, and you should be clothed in sincere compassion, in kindness and humility, gentleness and patience. Bear with one another; forgive each other as soon as a quarrel begins. The Lord has forgiven you; now you must do the same. Over all these clothes, to keep them together and complete them, put on love. And may the peace of Christ reign in your hearts; because it is for this that you are called together as parts of one body. Always be thankful. Colossians 3: 12 - 15

OLD TESTAMENT PASSAGES

St Jerome said that "ignorance of the Scriptures was ignorance of Christ". And he was not confining himself to the New Testament. Reflecting on these lines from the Old Testament can help nourish our devotion. They are simply an introduction to the limiless pastures of Sacred Scripture.

CRUSHED FOR OUR SINS

Yet he was pierced through for our faults, crushed for our sins.... and through his wounds we are healed. Isaiah 53: 5

OUR COMPASSIONATE LORD

O Lord you will not withhold your compassion from me. Your merciful love and your truth will always guard me. Ps 39:11-12

OUR SAVIOUR

Lord make me know your ways
Lord, teach me your paths
Make me walk in your truth and teach me for you are God my Saviour.
Ps 24: 4-5

THANKS TO THE FORGIVING LORD

My soul give thanks to the Lord
all my being, bless his holy name
My soul, give thanks to the Lord
and never forget all his blessings
It is he who forgives all your guilt
who heals every one of your ills,
who redeems your life from the grave,
who crowns you with love and compassion,
who renews your youth like the eagle's.

Ps 102: 1-4

GRATITUDE

How can I repay the Lord for his goodness to me?
I will take the cup of salvation,
I will call on God's name.
Ps 115:12

THE LORD IS CLOSE TO US

He is close to all who call him
who call on him from their hearts.
Ps 144:18

TRUST IN THE LORD

But as for me I trust in you, Lord.
I say: you are my God.
Ps 30 : 14

MY HELP

You have been my help
In the shadow of your wings I rejoice
My soul clings to you
Your right hand holds me fast.
Ps 62: 7-8

Chapter Five

Acts of
Consecration

Anything that denies self is an act of love.
Fr John Sullivan S.J., Servant of God (1861-1933)

On June 21st, 1675, St Margaret Mary Alacoque and St Claude la Colombière *consecrated themselves together to the Sacred Heart. This action, under the inspiration of the Sacred Heart Himself, who had just recently revealed Himself to St Margaret Mary, was a new departure in Christian spirituality. Before that, only Jesus had consecrated himself and, as we learn in John 17, he then consecrated his apostles. In subsequent Church practice consecration was always something which was done to a person by a hierarchical superior. The consecration of virgins by their bishop, a rite recently restored in the Church and which predates profession in a religious community as we have come to know it, was one of the first developments along this line. However, as a result of the inspired initiative of the two saints, personal consecration made its way into Catholic piety with individuals, families, cities and nations consecrating themselves to the Sacred Heart. The Pioneer Offering is an instance of a personal consecration to the Sacred Heart of one's right to drink. Here we present different instances of Acts of Consecration which members may find appropriate at different times in their lives.*

MORNING OFFERING
(Used in the Apostolate of Prayer)
O Jesus, through the most pure heart of Mary, I offer You all my prayers, works, joys and sufferings of this day in union with the Holy Sacrifice of the Mass throughout the world. I offer them for all the intentions of Your Sacred Heart: the salvation of souls, reparation for sin, the reunion of all Christians. I offer them for the intentions of our Bishops and of all our members, and in particular for those recommended by our Holy Father, for all the intentions of Your Divine Heart.

PERSONAL ACT OF CONSECRATION

Most Sacred Heart of Jesus, to You I, N........N........ devote and offer up my life, thoughts, words, actions, pains and sufferings. May the least part of my being be no longer employed save only in loving, serving, honouring and glorifying You. For this reason, O most Sacred Heart, be the sole object of my love, the protector of my life, the pledge of my salvation and my secure refuge at the hour of my death. May You be, O most bountiful Heart, my justification before the throne of God and screen me from His anger which I have so justly merited. In You I place all my confidence and convinced as I am of my own weakness, I rely entirely on Your bounty.

Annihilate in me all that is displeasing and offensive to Your pure eye. Imprint Yourself like a divine seal upon my heart that I may ever remember my obligation never to be separated from You. May my name also, I beseech You, by Your tender bounty, be written in You, O Book of Life, and may I ever be a victim, consecrated to Your glory, ever burning with the flames of Your pure love and entirely penetrated with it for all eternity. In this I place all my happiness, this is all my desire, to live and die in no other quality but that of Your devoted servant. Amen
(St Margaret Mary composed this prayer shortly after receiving her first revelations from the Sacred Heart)

ACT OF CONSECRATION OF THE FAMILY
TO THE SACRED HEART

O Sacred Heart of Jesus, who made known to St Margaret Mary Your great desire to reign over Christian families, we are gathered here today to proclaim Your complete dominion over our family. From now on we promise to lead a Christlike life: we will strive to develop in our home all the virtues which bring with them the peace that You promised. And we will not compromise with the spirit of secularism which You have so strongly denounced.

You will rule over our minds through our deep and living faith. You will be King of our hearts by our generous love for You; and we will cultivate this love by frequent reception of You in Holy Communion.

Divine Heart of Jesus, preside over our family gatherings; bless all our family undertakings,both spiritual and temporal. Sanctify our joys and comfort us in our sorrows. And if any member of our family should have the misfortune to offend You seriously, remind him, O Sacred Heart of Jesus, of Your infinite love and mercy for the penitent sinner.

And when the hour of separation comes, when death brings its sorrow into our family, whether we go or whether we stay, we will humbly accept Your divine will. And at the same time we will console and comfort ourselves with the thought that the time will come when our whole family will be united lovingly with You in heaven forever.

(All members of the family kneel and say in unison this Act before a picture or statue of the Sacred Heart)

AN ACT OF DEDICATION OF THE HUMAN RACE

Most kind Jesus, Redeemer of the human race, look down upon us humbly prostrate before Your altar (*outside a church or oratory say:* in your presence). We are Yours, and Yours we wish to be; but to be more surely united to You, behold, each one of us freely dedicates himself to Your most Sacred Heart. Many, indeed have never known You; many, too, despising Your precepts, have rejected You. Have mercy on them all, most merciful Jesus, and draw them to Your Most Sacred Heart.

Be King, O Lord, not only of the faithful who have never forsaken You, but also of the prodigal sons who have abandoned You: grant that they may quickly return to their Father's house, lest they perish of wretchedness and hunger.

Be King of those whom heresy holds in error or discord keeps aloof; call them back to the harbour of truth and the unity of faith, so that soon there may be but one fold and one Shepherd.

Grant, O Lord, to your Church, assurance of freedom and immunity from harm; unto all nations give an ordered tranquillity; bring it to pass that from pole to pole the earth may resound with one cry:

Praise to the divine Heart that wrought our salvation; to it be honour and glory for ever and ever. Amen.

Pope Leo XIII, May 25th 1899

SOLEMN ACT OF FAMILY DEDICATION

Lord Jesus Christ, we are gathered together today in your name. We believe you are present among us. We praise and thank you for all your goodness. You are seated in glory at the right hand of your Father and never cease to intercede for us. All our gifts are yours. We thank you for them all, especially for our love for one another, our home, our happiness. We wish in return to offer our lives to you by dedicating our family to your Sacred Heart. Be with us always, Lord, as the life and centre of our home.

You offered your life in sacrifice for all men and gave yourself to us in the Eucharist. United with you in baptism, we wish to live by your life, offering ourselves with you in the Mass, receiving you in Holy Communion, and turning to you in our family prayer. Through your Holy Spirit strengthen the ties which hold us, and keep us one with you in all our undertakings.

Watch over our family. Keep us from evil and from harm. Guide and bless all we do. Sanctify our joys, comfort us in our sufferings. In times of trial and sorrow help us to draw courage and hope from your cross and resurrection.

If ever we sin, grant us the grace to return to you in prayer and penance. Never let anger, resentment or bitterness take hold of us or a vindictive, unbending spirit be ours. Keep us one in love and make our hearts like yours-always open to others and ready to forgive.

Give us courage to face the changes and partings of this passing life. When death comes to our family, make us calm and strong in hope, submissive to your will and a comfort to one another. In that hour be very close to us. Trusting in your love may we learn to look forward in joyful hope to our reunion in Heaven, where we shall live together with you and the Father and the Holy Spirit forever.

Lord Jesus Christ, accept this dedication of our family to your Sacred Heart. Keep us in your love. May Mary your Mother and Saint Joseph help us to be true to what we promise you this day.

SHORTER ACT OF DEDICATION WHICH MAY BE USED FREQUENTLY.

Lord Jesus Christ, today we renew the dedication of our family to your Sacred Heart. We remember your love for us. We pledge our love in return, placing you at the centre of our hearts and of our home. We wish to live our lives in union with you and share your mission of love to all humanity. Lord Jesus Christ, accept this dedication and keep us always in your Sacred Heart. Amen.

ACT OF OBLATION TO THE MERCIFUL LOVE OF GOD
Offering of myself as a Victim of Holocaust to God's Merciful Love.

O my God! Most Blessed Trinity, I desire to love You and make You loved, to work for the glory of Holy Church by saving souls on earth and liberating those suffering in purgatory. I desire to accomplish Your will perfectly and to reach the degree of glory You have prepared for me in Your Kingdom. I desire, in a word, to be a saint, but feel my helplessness and I beg You, O my God! to be Yourself my Sanctity.

I offer You, too, all the merits of the saints, in heaven and on earth, their acts of love, and those of the holy angels. Finally I offer You, O Blessed Trinity! the love and merits of the Blessed Virgin, my dear Mother. It is to her I abandon my offering, begging her to present it to You. Her Divine Son, My beloved spouse, told us in the days of his mortal life "Whatsoever you ask in my name he will give it to you". I am certain, then, that You will grant my desires: I know, O my God that the more You want to give the more You make us desire. I feel in my heart immense desires and it is with confidence that I ask You to come and take possession of my soul. Ah! I cannot receive Holy Communion as often as I desire, but, Lord are You not all-powerful? Remain in me as in a tabernacle and never separate Yourself from Your little Victim.

I want to console You for the ingratitude of the wicked, and I beg of You to take away my freedom to displease You. If through weakness I sometimes fall, may Your divine glance cleanse my soul immediately, consuming my imperfections like the fire that transforms everything into itself.

I thank You, O my God! for all the graces You have granted me, especially the grace of making me pass through the crucible of suffering. It is with joy I shall contemplate You on the Last Day carrying the sceptre of the Cross. Since You deigned to give me a share in this very precious Cross, I hope in heaven to resemble You and to see shining in my glorified body the sacred image of Your Passion.

After earth's exile, I hope to go and enjoy You in the Fatherland, but I do not want to lay up merits in Heaven. I want to work for Your love alone with the one purpose of pleasing you, consoling Your Sacred Heart, and saving souls who will love You eternally.

In the evening of my life, I shall appear before You with empty hands, for I do not ask You, Lord, to count my works. All our justice is stained in Your eyes. I wish, then, to be clothed in Your own Justice and to receive from Your love the eternal possession of Yourself. I want no other Throne, no other Crown but You, my Beloved!

Time is nothing in Your eyes, and a single day is like a thousand years. You can, then, in one instant, prepare me to appear before You.

In order to live in one single act of perfect love, I offer myself as a Victim of Holocaust to Your Merciful Love, asking You to consume me incessantly, allowing the waves of infinite tenderness shut up within You to overflow into my soul, and that thus I may become a martyr of Your love, O my God!

May this martyrdom, after having prepared me to appear before You, finally cause me to die and may my soul take its flight without delay into the eternal embrace of Your Merciful Love.

I want, O my Beloved, at each beat of my heart to renew this offering to You an infinite number of times, until the shadows having disappeared I may be able to tell You of My Love in an Eternal Face to Face!

Saint Thérèse of the Child Jesus on June 9th, 1895

"A few days after my Oblation to God's Merciful Love, I had commenced in the choir the Way of the Cross, when I felt myself suddenly wounded by a dart of fire so ardent that I thought I should die".

Chapter Six

Wine in the Scriptures

God saw that it was good
Book of Genesis I

The goodness of everything created is asserted from the first chapter of the first book of the bible, Genesis. The author's use of the phrase "and God saw that it was good" after each episode of the creation, makes this clear. His fascinating account of how evil rears its ugly head does not prejudice his basic stance that everything created is good. Evil only arises with the abuse of the gift of free will. He knows from ordinary experience that there is evil in the world but never considers it as created by God. If there is evil connected with drinking it is not in the drink but in the heart of the one who abuses the drink. This set the tone for all the subsequent authors of Sacred Scripture who dealt with use, abuse of and abstinence from food and drink.

As part of the Judaeo -Christian tradition our basic stance towards wine, the fruit of the vine, must be positive. It has to be seen as a gift of God. The Psalmist was in no doubt about this. Addressing the Creator he says:

> From your high halls you water the mountains
> satisfying the earth with the fruit of your works:
> for cattle you make the grass grow
> and for people the plants they need,
>
> to bring forth food from the earth,
> and wine to cheer people's hearts,
> oil to make their faces glow,
> food to make them sturdy of heart.
> Ps 104, 15

In biblical tradition, the discovery of the vine is attributed to Noah. This happened no sooner than he had emerged from the ark. The text indicates that from the beginning it appeared to be a mixed blessing. Noah himself had the dubious distinction of being the first person to get drunk.

The sons of Noah who came out of the ark were Shem, Ham and Japheth- Ham being the father of Canaan. These three were Noah's sons, and from these the whole earth was peopled. Noah, a tiller of the soil, was the first to plant the vine. He drank some of the wine, and while he was drunk, he lay uncovered in his tent. Ham, father of Canaan, saw his father naked and told his two brothers outside. Shem and Japheth took a cloak and they both put it over their shoulders, and walking backwards, covered their father's nakedness; they kept their faces turned away, and they did not look at their father naked.

Genesis 9, 18 -23

Scripture takes a balanced approach alerting us to both the benefits and the dangers of wine.

THE BENEFITS

In the Scriptures wine was seen as a sign of prosperity

Honour Yahweh with what goods you have
and with the first-fruits of all your produce
then your barns will be filled with corn,
your vats overflowing with new wine
Proverbs 3, 9-10

It was also seen as something which could enhance life, if used with discretion. Ben Sira, the author of Ecclesiasticus, presents a most balanced case for careful use while at the same time deploring abuse

Do not play the valiant at your wine,
for wine has been the undoing of many.
The furnace proves the temper of steel,
and wine proves hearts in the drinking bouts of braggarts.
Wine gives life if drunk in moderation.
What is life without wine?
It was created to make people happy.
Drunk at the right time and in the right amount,
wine makes for a glad heart and a cheerful mind.
Bitterness of soul comes of wine drunk to excess
out of temper or bravado.
Drunkenness excites the stupid to a fury to his own
harm, it reduces his strength while leading to blows.
Do not provoke your fellow-guest at a wine feast,
do not make fun of him when he is enjoying himself,
do not take him to task
or annoy him by reclaiming money owed.
Ecclesiasticus 31, 30-42

In the pastoral epistles of the New Testament there are many references to moderation. The leader in the Church assembly "must be temperate, discreet and courteous, hospitable and a good teacher; not a heavy drinker, nor hot-tempered, but gentle and peaceable, not avaricious." (1 Timothy 3,3) and again, deacons " must be respectable, not double-tongued, moderate in the amount of wine they drink and with no squalid greed for money" (1 Tim, 3,8). In 1 Timothy 5, 23, perhaps the most quoted text on the matter, Paul gives his advice to Timothy : " You should give up only drinking water and have a little wine for the sake of your digestion and frequent bouts of illness that you have". The generally accepted interpretation of this text by commentators from the time of St John Chrysostom until the present is that Timothy was living a life of fasting, something of which Paul approved. However, for reasons of health, he advises Timothy to mitigate his fast. Perhaps this is an instance of the situation envisaged by the Pioneer rule whereby members are permitted and indeed on occasion, exhorted, to follow the doctor's advice to take liquids with an alcohol content in a case of illness. Jesus Himself drank wine even at the risk of appearing in a bad light. He reacted strongly when both his own way of life and that of John the Baptist were interpreted in a mean-spirited way.

"What comparison can I find for this generation ? It is like children shouting to each other as they sit in the market place:

> We played the pipes for you,
> and you wouldn't dance;
> we sang dirges,
> and you wouldn't be mourners.

For John came, neither eating nor drinking, and they say,"He is possessed." The Son of Man came, eating and drinking, and they say, "Look, a glutton and a drunkard, a friend of tax-collectors and sinners." Yet wisdom is justified by her deeds. Matthew 11, 16-19

In the market place at Jerusalem children played a game called "weddings and funerals". The boys pretended to play the pipes and the girls were expected to dance. Then it was the turn of the girls to lament or "keen" and the boys were expected to weep. Jesus condemned his contemporaries for refusing to play either game. The austere, penitential life of John the Baptist without "wine or strong drink", already laid out for him before his birth (Luke 1,15), was rejected as a sign of diabolical possession. The willingness of Jesus to share the innocent pleasures of ordinary life was written off as drunkenness and gluttony. His approval, however, of the abstinence of the Baptist is obvious in the context.

DANGERS

Throughout their writings, the prophets denounce leaders who overdrink and consequently neglect their duties to God and those in their charge. Amos, the prophet of social justice, castigated leaders, one of whose crimes was "drinking the wine of the people they have fined in the house of their god" Amos 2,8. They were imposing exorbitant taxes on the people in order to fund this drinking and a luxurious life style. Hosea, the prophet of God's tender love, deplores the fact that "ministers become inflamed with wine" (Hosea, 7,5). In several places in his writings Isaiah vents his ire on leaders so preoccupied with drink that they think of nothing else. This preoccupation is symptomatic of irresponsibility and self-indulgence which will one day lead to the collapse of the nation and deportation to Babylon.

> "Woe to those who get up early to go after strong drink
> and stay up late at night inflamed with wine.
> Nothing but harp and lyre, tambourine and pipe,
> and wine for their drinking bouts.
> Never a thought for the works of Yahweh
> never a glance for what his hands have done
> Isaiah, 5,11,12

> "Woe to the haughty crown of Ephraim's drunkards
> to the fading flower of its proud splendour
> sited at the head of the lush valley,
> to those prostrated by wine!
> Isaiah 28,1

> "Its watchmen are all blind,
> they know nothing.
> Dumb watchdogs all, unable to bark,
> they dream, lie down, and love to sleep.
> Greedy dogs, never satisfied, such are the shepherds,
> who understand nothing;
> they all go their own way,
> each to the last man after his own interest.
> 'Come, let me fetch wine;
> We will get drunk on strong drink,
> tomorrow will be just as wonderful as today
> and even more so!'
> Isaiah, 56, 10-12

Whereas the prophets were concerned about the effects of overdrinking on the life of the nation, the writers of the books of wisdom noted the deplorable outcome of heavy drinking for the individual.

> "Pleasure-lovers stay poor,
> no one will grow rich who loves wine and good living.
> Proverbs 21,17

> "A drunken workman will never grow rich
> and one who makes light of small matters will gradually sink.
> Wine and women corrupt intelligent men

the customer of whores loses all sense of shame.
Ecclesiasticus 19,1,2

"Do not be one of those forever tippling wine
nor one of those who gorge themselves with meat;
for the drunkard and glutton impoverish themselves,
and sleepiness is clothed in rags.
Proverbs 23, 20,21

"For whom is pity, for whom contempt,
for whom is strife, for whom complaint,
for whom blows struck at random,
for whom the clouded eye?
For those who linger over wine too long,
ever on the look-out for blended liquors.
Do not gaze at wine, how red it is,
how it sparkles in the cup !
How smoothly it slips down the throat!
In the end its bite is like a serpent's,
its sting as sharp as an adder's.
Your eyes will see peculiar things,
you will talk nonsense from your heart.
You will be like someone sleeping in mid-ocean,
like one asleep at the mast-head.
'Struck me, have they ? But I'm not hurt.
Beaten me ? I don't feel anything.
When shall I wake up ?
I'll ask for more of it !"
Proverbs 23, 29-35

St Paul was in no doubt about the serious consequences of drunkenness.
"So be very careful about the sort of lives you lead,
like intelligent and not like senseless people. Make
the best use of the present time, for it is a wicked age.
This is why you must not be thoughtless but must
recognise what is the will of the Lord. Do not get
drunk with wine; this is simply dissipation; be filled
with the Spirit.
Eph 5, 18

When writing to the Galatians, St Paul warned them that drunkenness could jeopardise one's salvation.
"When self-indulgence is at work the results are
obvious: sexual vice, impurity, and sensuality, the
worship of false gods and sorcery; antagonisms and
rivalry, jealousy, bad temper and quarrels,

disagreements, factions and malice, drunkenness, orgies
and such things. And about these, I tell you now as I
have told you in the past, that people who behave in
these ways will not inherit the kingdom of God.
Galatians 5, 18 -21

WINE IN THE LIFE OF WORSHIP

Wine has always been used in sacrifice and worship in the Judaeo-Christian
tradition. There are references to its use in libations (Hosea 9,4) and as part of
the first-fruits to be given to the priests

You must give him the first-fruits
of your wheat, of your new wine
and of your oil, as well as
the first fruits of your sheep shearing.
Dt.18, 4

At the marriage feast at Cana it would be the sign of joy now become a reality
by the presence among us of the Messiah. The new wine is the symbol of
Messianic times.

However, there is ample evidence in the scriptures of religious motivation
causing some to abstain from wine. These included priests, judges, prophets,
ordinary Israelites and in the case of the Rechabites, a whole clan.
Priests were forbidden to drink wine at certain times:

Yahweh spoke to Aaron and said:
"When you come to the Tent of Meeting, you and your
sons with you, you may not drink wine or any other
fermented liquor, to avoid incurring death. This is a
perpetual law for your descendants. And so it shall be
also when you separate the sacred from the profane, the
unclean from the clean, and when you teach the
Israelites any of the decrees that Yahweh has
pronounced for them through Moses.
Leviticus 10, 8-11

The mother of Samson received a clear message from the angel who foretold
the birth of her son that she must observe the rules of the nazarite that will
later bind her son.

"You are barren and have had no child, but you are
going to conceive and give birth to a son. From now on,
take great care. From now on, drink no wine or
fermented liquor, and eat nothing unclean. For the boy
is to be God's nazarite from his mother's womb to his
dying day."
Judges 13,3-5

This is in line with the teaching of Moses on the Nazarite, (from the Hebrew nâzîr: set apart, consecrated), part of whose vow entailed abstention from drink, indicating a willingness to forego a life of ease (cf. relevant footnote in the New Bible of Jerusalem).

> Yahweh spoke to Moses and said, Speak to the
> Israelites and say:
> "If a man or a woman wishes to make a vow, the
> nazarite vow, to vow himself to Yahweh, he will
> abstain from wine and fermented liquor, he will
> not drink vinegar derived from one or the other, he
> will not drink grape-juice or eat grapes, be they
> fresh or dried. For the duration of his vow he will
> eat nothing that comes from the vine, not even juice
> of unripe grapes or skins of grapes."
> Numbers 6, 1-5

Jeremiah admired the religiously motivated abstinence and austere life of the Rechabites. When this nomadic clan came into the city of Jerusalem to escape the armies of the Chaldaeans and the Aramaeans, the Lord told Jeremiah to bring them into one of the rooms of the Temple and offer them wine to drink, which he duly did. Their reaction to this offer would teach Jeremiah in a peculiar way how highly the Lord values obedience to his word:

> "I then set pitchers full of wine, and some cups before
> the members of the Rechabite clan and said, drink some
> wine.'
> But they replied, 'We do not drink wine, because our
> ancestor Jonadab son of Rechab gave us this order,
> "You must not drink wine, neither you nor your sons for
> ever; nor must you live in houses, sow seed, plant
> vineyards or own them, but must live in tents all
> your lives, so that you may live long on the soil to
> which you are alien." We have punctiliously obeyed
> the order of our ancestor, Jonadab son of Rechab, never
> drinking wine ourselves, nor our wives, our sons or our
> daughters, not building houses to live in, owning
> neither vineyard nor field nor seed, living in tents. We
> have obeyed the orders of our ancestor Jonadab
> respecting them in every particular. However when
> Nebuchadnezzar king of Babylon invaded this country, we
> decided, "We must get away! We will go to Jerusalem to

escape the armies of the Chaldaeans and Aramaeans." So
that is why we are living in Jerusalem.'
Then the word of Yahweh came to Jeremiah as follows,
'Yahweh Sabaoth, the God of Israel says this,"Go and
say to the people of Judah and the inhabitants of
Jerusalem: Will you never learn the lesson and listen
to my words,Yahweh demands? The words of Jonadab son of
Rechab, ordering his sons to drink no wine, have been
observed; obedient to their ancestors' command, they
drink none even today. But to me, who spoke so
urgently, so untiringly, you have not listened. I have
urgently and untiringly sent you all my servants the
prophets to say: Turn back, each one of you, from your
evil behaviour and amend your actions, do not follow
other gods to serve them, and you will go on living on
the soil I gave your ancestors. But you have not paid
attention or listened to me. Thus the sons of Jonadab
son of Rechab have kept the command their ancestor gave
them, but this people has not listened to me. And so,
Yahweh Sabaoth, God of Israel, says this: Look, on
Judah and the citizens of Jerusalem I am going to bring
all the disaster which I decreed for them, because I
spoke to them and they would not listen, called to them
and they would not answer.'"
Then Jeremiah said to the Rechabite clan, 'Yahweh
Sabaoth, the God of Israel, says this, "Because you
have obeyed the orders of your ancestors Jonadab and
observed all his rules and done everything he ordered
you to do, therefore, Yahweh Sabaoth, the God of
Israel, says this: Jonadab son of Rechab will never
lack a male descendant to stand before me for ever."'
Jeremiah 35, 6-19

The faithful were often encouraged in post-exilic Judaism to renounce wine to
avoid any danger of compromise with paganism as can be found in the quaint
story where Daniel and his companions refused the royal wine and after only
eating vegetables and drinking water for ten days "they looked better and fatter
than any of the boys who had eaten their allowance from the royal table".
(Daniel 1.)

THE SYMBOLISM OF WINE
From a profane point of view, wine is the symbol of everything that is pleasant
in life. For instance,in the Song of Songs it represents human love " How
delicious is your love, more delicious than wine" (Song 4,10). However it can

also call to mind deplorable drunkenness, "Babylon was a golden cup in Yahweh's hand, she made the whole world drunk, the nations drank her wine and then went mad." (Jr 51,7).

From a religious point of view, being deprived of wine can symbolise divine displeasure, " although you planted pleasant vineyards, you will not drink wine from them for I know how many are your crimes" (Am 5,11). The only wine available then is the wine of the divine wrath, "To your feet, Jerusalem! You who from Yahweh's hand have drunk the cup of wrath, the chalice, the stupefying cup, you have drained to the dregs" (Is 51,17). But then the happiness God promises is expressed in terms of an abundance of wine, "On this mountain, for all peoples, Yahweh Sabaoth is preparing a banquet of rich food, a banquet of fine wines, of succulent food, of well-strained wines." (Is.25,6)

In the New Testament, the "new wine" is the symbol of Messianic times. It will burst the old wine skins and usher in a whole new era in human life that will only reach its completion in the heavenly banquet. But the mention of wine in the New Testament becomes much more than simply symbolic as Jesus will actually give his blood under the appearance of wine. The life of each Christian will be nourished by the wine turned to blood.

CONCLUSION

In Judaeo-Christianity the norm in adult life has always been to take wine. It goes without saying that this implied moderation. Excess, which the prophets excoriated, was out of the question. Complete renunciation, however, was frequently the choice of outstanding figures, both men and women, in the history of salvation. As a sign of their consecration in response to divine inspiration they freely renounced the pleasure attaching to wine. Pioneers, in restricting their use of wine to its place in the Eucharistic sacrifice, situate themselves in this long and honourable tradition..

Chapter Seven

Saintly Members of the Pioneer Association

The causes for the canonisation of a number of Pioneers are already in process: Venerable Matt Talbot, Venerable Edel Quinn, and the Servants of God, Fr John Sullivan and Frank Duff. Fr Willie Doyle, S.J., who was killed in 1917 in World War 1 and whose sanctity was generally recognised, was a member of the Central Council at the time of his death.

VENERABLE MATT TALBOT

Venerable Matt Talbot was born at Dublin in 1856, the year Fr Theobold Mathew, the great Apostle of Temperance, died. The message of Fr Mathew had had very little influence in the Talbot family where heavy drinking seemed to be part of life. Matt started drinking while still a youngster. It eventually came to dominate his whole life until his dramatic conversion in 1884. He was penniless and hoping that his friends would buy him a drink. In his bitter disappointment when they ignored him the grace of God touched his heart. He realised that he just had to give up drink and so took the pledge. Matt not only made a virtue of a necessity but made it the first step to great sanctity. Shortly after making the break with drink he undertook a life of prayer and fasting which he sustained heroically until the end of his life. He later confided to friends that he had found it harder to give up cigarettes than drink. In 1891 he joined a total abstinence group which later developed into the fully-formed Pioneer Association. He died in Granby Lane, Dublin on his way to Mass at St Saviour's Dominican Church on Trinity Sunday, 1925.

Within days of his death people were making their way to his tomb. Eventually the cause for his canonisation was introduced. He was declared a Servant of God and later Venerable, which means that he practised the theological virtue of faith, hope and charity as well as the cardinal virtues of prudence, justice, fortitude and temperance to a heroic degree. His remains are venerated at a Shrine in Our Lady of Lourdes Church, Sean McDermott Street, Dublin.

PRAYER FOR THE CANONISATION OF VENERABLE MATT TALBOT

Lord, in your servant Matt Talbot you have given us a wonderful example of triumph over addiction, of devotion to duty, and of lifelong reverence for the Most Holy Sacrament. May his life of prayer and penance give us courage to take up our crosses and follow in the footsteps of Our Lord and Saviour, Jesus Christ.

Father, if it be your will that your beloved servant should be glorified by your Church, make known by your heavenly favours the power he enjoys in your sight. We ask this through the same Jesus Christ Our Lord.

VENERABLE EDEL QUINN

Venerable Edel Quinn (1907-1944) was born in Kanturk in Co. Cork, Ireland and died of tuberculosis at Nairobi, Kenya in 1944. A high-spirited young woman, she volunteered to go to East Africa as an envoy of the Legion of Mary where her labours and efforts in the cause of Christ became legendary. In spite of her illness she travelled thousands of miles to launch praesidia of the Legion. Her love for the Sacred Heart was apparent in her unremitting efforts to make him known. Like so many of the early Legionaries she became a Pioneer. She made an indelible impression on everyone she met by her selflessness and zeal for the things of God.

She had suffered from tuberculosis before even setting out for Africa. While there, during the Second World War, she contracted malaria. In spite of this she battled on valiantly, undertaking long, difficult journeys. Eventually worn out by her strenuous labours she died on May 12th, 1944 in Nairobi, where she is buried. The late Leon-Joseph Cardinal Suenens brought her name to the attention of a world-wide audience with his masterly biography *"A Life of Edel Quinn, a heroine of the apostolate"*, published in English in 1953. After exhaustive examination she was declared Venerable by Pope John Paul II in 1995.

PRAYER FOR THE CANONIZATION OF VENERABLE EDEL QUINN

Eternal Father, I thank you for the grace you gave to your servant, Edel Quinn, of striving to live always in the joy of your presence, for the radiant charity infused in her heart by your Holy Spirit, and for the strength she drew from the Bread of Life to labour until death for the glory of your name, in loving dependence on Mary, Mother of the Church.

Confident, O Merciful Father, that her life was pleasing to you, I beg you to grant me, through her intercession, the special favour I now implore....... and to make known by miracles the glory she enjoys in Heaven, so that she may be glorified also by your Church on earth, through Christ our Lord. Amen.

This prayer was composed by a Cardinal Archbishop of Quito, Equador on reading the biography by Cardinal Suenens.

THE SERVANT OF GOD, FATHER JOHN SULLIVAN, S.J.

The Servant of God, John Sullivan S.J. (1861-1933) was raised as a member of the Church of Ireland. After a course of studies at Trinity College, Dublin, he qualifed as a barrister. On December 21st 1896, he was received into the Catholic Church in London at Farm Street Jesuit Church and a few years later in Ireland he entered the Society of Jesus at Tullamore on September 7th, 1900. The intensity with which he embraced the religious life became very obvious to all who knew him from his first days in the novitiate. As a priest he was known for his love of the sick and was indefatigable in visiting them in hospitals and their homes. Many cures were reported after his prayerful visits. He led a most abstemious and mortified life. A firm believer in the spiritual benefits of Pioneer membership he encouraged many of the boys in his care to become members. The Pioneer pin which he himself wore faithfully during his life is preserved in Clongowes Wood College, Co Kildare, where he ministered for the greater part of his priestly life.

He died in 1933 with a reputation for great holiness. In 1960, his remains were brought to the Church of St Francis Xavier, Dublin (where the Pioneer Association was founded) and placed in a specially prepared tomb beside the Chapel of the Sacred Heart.

PRAYER FOR THE CANONISATION OF FR JOHN SULLIVAN, S.J.

O God, who honour those who honour you, make sacred the memory of your servant, John Sullivan, by granting through his intercession the petition we now make (*specify the petition*) and hastening the day when his name will be numbered among those of your saints. We make our prayer through Christ our Lord. Amen

(For the purposes of novenas, one Our Father and Hail Mary and Glory be to the Father may be added in honour of the Passion and Resurrection of Our Lord to which Fr John was particularly devoted).

THE SERVANT OF GOD, FRANK DUFF

The Servant of God, Frank Duff (1889 - 1980) founded the Legion of Mary in 1921. He had joined the Pioneer Association some years previously and was firmly convinced of its apostolic value. The men and women who were present at the foundation meeting of the Legion were all Pioneers. Throughout his long life he encouraged the Legion to promote the Pioneer Association.

On July 16th, 1996, Archbishop Desmond Connell of Dublin accepted and signed the official petition to introduce the cause for the Beatification of Frank Duff. The Archbishop said that it was a truly historic occasion and that he was privileged to introduce the Cause in the Archdiocese. He invited members of the faithful to report to the Archdiocese any useful information which may concern the cause.

PRAYER FOR THE BEATIFICATION OF FRANK DUFF

God our Father,

You inspired your servant Frank Duff with a profound insight into the mystery of your Church, the Body of Christ, and of the place of Mary the Mother of Jesus in this mystery.

In his immense desire to share this insight with others and in filial dependence on Mary he formed her Legion to be a sign of her maternal love for the world and a means of enlisting all her children in the Church's evangelising work.

We thank you Father for the graces conferred on him and for the benefits accruing to the Church from his courageous and shining faith.

With confidence we beg you that through his intercession you grant the petition we lay before you.......

We ask too that, if it be in accordance with your will, the holiness of his life may be acknowledged by the Church for the glory of your Name, through Christ our Lord. Amen.

FR WILLIAM DOYLE, S.J. (1873-1917)

Fr William (Willie) Doyle was killed in the First World War on August 16th, 1917 while trying to minister to wounded men during fierce fighting in Flanders. His body was never found. At the time of his death, along with Fr Cullen, the founder and two other Jesuits, he was a member of the small Central Council of the Pioneer Association. He was idolized by men of all religions who witnessed his extraordinary bravery and self-sacrifice. Within a few years of his death, Alfred O'Rahilly had written his biography. This book, one of the finest on a religious theme published in Ireland in the 20th century, went into several editions and brought Fr Doyle's name to the attention of a worldwide audience.

In the years following his death there was widespread devotion to him and numerous favours and cures were attributed to his intercession.

Chapter Eight

Our Lady in
Pioneer Spirituality

To carry on its important work, the Pioneer Association, like every other religious organisation, has to continually face a two-fold challenge: to adapt appropriately to changing circumstances and at the same time to remain faithful to the original charism of its founder. After the Second Vatican Council, one of the great turning points in modern church history, Pope Paul VI invited all existing religious groups to take adaptation seriously but to do so in the spirit of their founder. They were to make a special effort to understand more profoundly what he called the "charism" of their congregation or association, to be found in a special way in the life and practice of the founder. In the Pioneer Association, the extensive writings, both by and about the founder, Fr Cullen, have facilitated this process. From the "Life of Fr Cullen" by Fr Lambert McKenna, it is obvious that his Pioneer work was simply an extension of his great love for the Sacred Heart. What also emerges from Fr McKenna's biography is that for Fr Cullen devotion to the Mother of God was an integral part of this devotion to her Son. In this, his Marian approach is reminiscent of the extraordinary Marian devotion that would one day characterize the papacy of Pope John Paul 11. To be faithful to the charism of their founder, Pioneers must give Mary a very special place in their hearts. The following extracts from Fr McKenna's biography are most revealing about Fr Cullen's mind on the matter.

FR CULLEN'S PLEDGE TAKEN IN HONOUR OF OUR LADY OF THE ROSARY

Fr Cullen was ten years a priest before he became convinced that all other expedients (to deal with drink abuse) were failures, and was driven to try once more the much-decried one of Fr Mathew. In October, 1874, he was engaged in giving a mission in Glynn, Co Wexford, when in the sacristy during his thanksgiving after Mass on Rosary Sunday, he resolved "to imitate, however feebly, the great example of Father Mathew" and to pledge himself never to touch stimulants for the rest of his life.

"At this time" he says," this step was very unusual. I knew its prudence would be challenged, and its utility denied; but I placed my hope in Our Lady of the Rosary, she of whom it has never been heard in any age that she abandoned those who sought her help".

The pledge then taken he kept faithfully to the end. He never could be induced to break it, even during one of his voyages across the ocean when the doctor told him that spirits were necessary to preserve his life; nor afterwards, when in his travels through Africa he found nothing but evil smelling water to drink.

TENDERNESS OF HIS LOVE FOR MARY

Love not merely unites souls but makes them like each other. Two loving souls will tend to have the same thoughts and desires. And so Fr Cullen, whose mind was set steadily on Christ's interests, and whose heart was set on wishing and loving what Christ wished and loved, could not but have a tender love for Christ's mother. This love of Mary took possession of his heart even when he was a small child. The Hail Holy Queen was one of his favourite prayers even then, and he tells us that from his earliest years he had acquired the habit of saying every day three Hail Marys in honour of the Immaculate Conception - a habit to which he attributed in great measure his having been kept from serious sin all his life, and one which he never omitted to recommend to all young boys with whom he came in contact. He records at the end of one of his retreats "an extraordinary increase in a grace which has grown unconsciously and very slowly, the grace of easily turning to my Mother Mary in all my troubles. I devoutly love her. She fills my whole life. I feel her sweet presence as a golden haze of warmth and love around me." "O Mother, I cast myself and all that I have into thy arms, into thy holy heart. Keep me and mine during life and at death in that holy tabernacle. I don't know what to ask thee for most, or what most to thank thee for, my dearest Mother!" A convert lady told him one time that she had never cared for the excessive attention and love devoted by born Catholics to the Blessed Virgin. "Gracious!" he said, "if I did not look forward to seeing Mary in Heaven, I would not long for it as I do; I would not feel it to be my home !"

TURNING TO MARY WHEN TROUBLED

In particular did he turn to Mary in times of trouble. During a long period lasting over years when he was suffering intensely from a domestic trouble, every single day he renewed his appeal to Mary: " Am I to be the first thou didst forget ?" "I beseech thee not to forget thy child of the Memorare. I find it very hard to bear my cross patiently. Help me to bear it still. I cannot of myself. Help me to bear it, or rather if it be God's will, take it from me. Have I not worked for thee all my life, my Mother, and wilt thou now reject me ! Never" And again: "O dearest Mother Mary, my own blessed and all-powerful Mother, I place myself kneeling at thy feet. I see thee near to me. Thou didst say to me; 'Ego ero tecum' (I will be with you) I know not how thou intendest to come. All I know is that thou sayest that thou art very near to me, and that I do not implore thee in vain, and that I shall not be the first to call on thee and be rejected".

MARY, HEALTH OF THE SICK

The reference in these words "Ego ero tecum" (which he placed for years at the top of every page of his Diary) is to an experience of his at Lourdes in 1875: " Remember, how twenty-eight years ago, I assisted at thy crowning at Lourdes, and how, when I was desolate and embarrassed, thou didst comfort me by saying to me in my soul interiorly: "Ego ero tecum"- those words which ever since have been my watchword, giving me confidence unfailing." In his lesser troubles of pain or sickness, too, he had recourse to Mary, and, on at least one occasion, seemed to himself to hear her words. He refers to it thus: "O my Divine Jesus, cure my chest and cough. Thy Mother Mary told me (I thought) that 'she would make me stronger than ever'".

This assurance of her help was not the only favour which he considered he received at the hands of the Blessed Virgin of Lourdes. For two years before 1896 he had been suffering very much from his ankle. Though he was able to get about, and in fact continued his missionary activities as usual, he was constantly in very acute pain. He had consulted three doctors, but had not been benefitted by their advice. He determined to go to Lourdes. Before going, he asked the Blessed Virgin to cure him outright - or at least to send him to someone who would cure him. At Lourdes, in spite of his prayer, he felt no relief, but did not give up hope, even when on his return the pain continued as severe as ever. One day,when limping along the road in the outskirts of Enniscorthy, a poor man - a cow-doctor - whom he met expressed some sympathy with him for his lameness. Feeling sure his prayer was about to be answered, he asked this man for a cure. The man gave him some stuff to put on his ankle, and told him to go to bed for a week, at the end of which time he would be cured. Fr Cullen took the stuff, used it as he was directed, and went to bed. At the end of the week he rose up perfectly cured. He used to tell the story afterwards, giving it for what it was worth, but declaring that, for his part, he believed firmly that the Blessed Virgin had thus heard his prayer and had cured him.

HIS LOVE FOR MARIAN SHRINES

He had a special attraction for the shrines of Mary - greatest, of course, for her greatest shrines, those of Loreto and Lourdes (on the latter of which he constantly gave a lecture with lantern-slides) - but also for the shrine in Lady's Island, Co Wexford, which he visited whenever he was in the neighbourhood. All his friends knew he constantly visited the Shrine of Our Lady in the Augustinian Church, Thomas Street, Dublin - a "little pilgrimage" which he recommended to all his poor friends who could not visit Mary's greater shrines of Loreto and Lourdes.

THE PLACE OF THE ROSARY IN HIS LIFE

As for the Rosary taught him by his mother and said by him every day during his school-days, he writes in 1915: "My Rosary-beads are my great hope. Wilfully I do not remember ever during my life missing it. Blessed be thou for this". In another place we find: "O my dearest Mother of my God, I beg of thee to enable me to say my Rosary with real love and affection. Make each Our Father to be a red rose, each Hail Mary a white rose, and each Gloria Patri a golden rose, piled round thy feet." And, again (October 1st, 1910): "O my sweetest Mother, bless me in this first day of your own sweet Rosary-month. What blessings it has brought me, my rosary-beads! It is my companion by day and night, on land and on sea, in joy and in sorrow. I expect every blessing to come to me through it, above all at the hour of my death." And then he recalled how it had saved a poor priest who had gone astray, and whom he had prepared for death. "Poor Father .... told me how his mother came to him just as he came out from the chapel after his ordination, and asked him to promise to say every day of his priestly life the Fifteen Decades of the Rosary. She died shortly after. He, in a chequered life at home and abroad, kept his promise, never omitting the Rosary even at night in cold latitudes when the deck of the ship was covered in sleet and ice. O my Mother of the Rosary, when shall I meet thee, and give into thy hands my Rosary-beads to be blessed for all eternity?"

ACT OF CONSECRATION TO OUR LADY

O Mary, my mother and my queen,
I consecrate myself to you forever
and without any reserve.
I abandon into your hands
the past, the present and the future.
Under your powerful protection
I wish to begin, to continue and to end all my actions.
Your name, O Mary, shall be my prayer.
I will say it in my joys and in my sorrows,
in my temptations and in my difficulties.
Yes, I will repeat it a hundred times a day.
And when my dying lips can no longer pronounce it,
my heart will still echo it with renewed
love and confidence, even to my last sigh:
O Mary conceived without sin,
pray for us who have recourse to you.
Amen.

SECTION TWO:
Gatherings of the Association

Chapter Nine

Meetings, Ceremonies and Initiation of Youth

COMING TOGETHER AS PIONEERS

Fr Cullen was convinced that the regular monthly meeting of the Council at local Centre level was essential for the survival of the Pioneer Association. He envisaged this as a meeting of about ten or twelve people who would oversee Pioneer activities in the parish and liaise with the Central Office. It was not his intention that all Pioneers attend these meetings as a condition of membership. He was confident, however, that a sufficient number of Pioneers would go beyond the call of duty and take responsibility for a Council, ensuring a monthly meeting in their local centre. It is this generosity and dedication which keeps the Pioneer ideal alive.

Besides these monthly meetings, there has been a tradition from the beginning of promoting events of all kinds, aimed at building up a Pioneer spirit and consolidating the strength of the membership. These began with Fr Cullen himself who was a great believer in bringing people together for mutual support. He revealed his mind on the matter in a lecture given to students at All Hallows' College, Dublin. "Since I started- principally with your help- the Pioneer Association more than six years ago, the imperative need of more wholesome recreations and amusements for our people, young and old, has been forcing itself upon me. I feel, too, that the Pioneers, now nearly 40,000 in number, have almost a claim in justice and charity to assistance in this matter from those who have urged them to join the movement. They have a right to say: 'Under your guidance, we have voluntarily renounced the use of alcoholic drink, even its moderate use; we have thereby surrendered what to already sober men was a perfectly lawful pleasure. Is it not reasonable to expect from you, who have counselled us to sacrifice this harmless enjoyment, that you provide us with some substitute?"

Pioneer leaders have responded admirably through the years to this challenge, issued in the early years of the 20th century. They have organised all sorts of alternative events, ranging from small intimate gatherings in private homes to the huge Diamond Jubilee Rally in 1959, described by Cardinal Conway as "a hosting of eternity" when almost 115,000 people assembled in Croke Park, Dublin.   As a religiously   motivated association, the main emphasis however, is on the spiritual aspects of abstinence and on giving it expression in Catholic devotional practices. Over the years this has involved enthusiastic participation in Church-based events like Masses, pilgrimages and different types of para-liturgical ceremonies. This is very much in the spirit of Fr Cullen who made a pilgrimage to the Shrine of St Patrick, Lough Derg, County Donegal, a few short months before founding the Association.

PRAYERFUL GATHERINGS

While there may be less need nowadays to provide alternative recreation for people, given the plethora of possibilities on offer, there is still need to promote the spiritual dimension of the Association with renewed vigour. To do this effectively is a great challenge. For this reason, local Councils should occasionally invite people to pray with them to the Sacred Heart, "the abyss of all virtues", for the spread of sobriety. A prayerful gathering of Pioneers and their friends could not but be of benefit to any parish. Some of the material in this book could be helpful in running such a prayer service.

Suggested Format for a Prayer Service

1. Opening prayer to the Holy Spirit for guidance.
2. Short talk or Reading from this book or other appropriate material.
3. Sharing of personal experience. Pioneers should not be reticent about telling others about God's goodness to them. They should take as addressed to themselves the words of the New Testament: "Do not drug yourselves with wine; this is simply dissipation; be filled with the Spirit. Sing psalms and hymns and inspired songs among yourselves, singing and chanting to the Lord in your hearts, always and everywhere giving thanks to God who is our Father in the name of Our Lord Jesus Christ." Ephesians, 5,18-20.
4. Prayers arising from the sharing.
5. Acts of Consecration. A choice may be found in chapter four.
6. Recitation in common of the Heroic Offering
7. A hymn.

MARKING STAGES OF COMMITMENT

Membership of the Pioneer Association is a public act. This is marked when a person joins or reaches a distinctive point such as 25 or 50 years of membership or when members simply wish to renew their pledge at a Pioneer gathering.

One of the three undertakings of membership, according to the mind of the founder, is the public wearing of a simple emblem of the Sacred Heart of Jesus. It is recommended to make the most of this as a parish event by holding an Enrolment Ceremony.

Enrolment Ceremony

Priest: Lord God, bless these badges, fashioned to recall your unfailing love for all of us. Bless those who will wear them and grant that they will remain faithful to their Pioneer pledge.

(Bless with Holy Water)

Name.....................Do you undertake to fulfill your commitment as a Pioneer?

Response: I do

Distribution: Receive this emblem of the Heart of Jesus. May you be faithful to the promise which you make today in response to His great love. We ask this through Christ our Lord.

Renewal Ceremony

This is recommended after the homily at a Mass where the celebrant asks these questions of those who are renewing their Pioneer promises:

1. Do you renew the promises of your Pioneer Offering to the Sacred Heart ?
   Response: I do.

2. Do you offer your pledge as an act of reparation to the Heart of Jesus?
   Response: I do.

3. Do you promise to offer your prayer and abstinence to win grace and help for people suffering from alcohol and substance abuse?
   Response: I do.

4. Do you promise to remain faithful to your Pioneer pledge all the days of your life ?
   Response: I do.

CELEBRANT: LET US PRAY.

Lord Jesus, each one of us gathered here together in your name is deeply conscious that our membership of the Pioneer Association is something special and important in our lives. We thank you for the privilege of being Pioneers and for the many blessings that have come to us through our membership. We ask you to grant us the grace of perseverance in our commitment and for help to serve you more generously. Bless the work of the Association, bless each one of us and help us give more effective witness to your love, for you live and reign for ever and ever. Amen

Priest blesses the members with holy water.

All together now recite the Pioneer Offering.

Jubilarian Ceremony

The blessing of the Jubilarian emblems precedes their distribution.

Priest: Receive this emblem of the Sacred Heart of Jesus as a token of your fidelity.

Prayer: Lord God, we thank you for granting *name* ....the grace of perseverance. We thank you too for the good that you have enabled him (her) to do for your cause. Continue to bless him (her) in his (her) efforts to work for your glory. We ask this through Christ our Lord.

INITIATION OF YOUTH

Ever since the beginning it has been part of the Pioneer way to introduce children to the ideal of self-sacrifice and the value of prayer for others. It is never too soon to begin this work. However, the presentation of the message must be adapted to the capacity of the children. In the Association there are three categories of youth membership: Juvenile (9 years +), Junior (12 years +) and more recently, Young Pioneers (15 years +). The three-fold commitment of· twice daily prayer, abstinence from alcohol and public wearing of the emblem applies to all three sections. The hope is that a significant number of these young people will one day graduate to the ranks of permanent lifelong Pioneers.

JUVENILE PIONEERS

The main objective of the Juvenile section, which caters for children aged 9 to 12, the three last years of primary education in most parts of the world, is to preserve them from ill-advised experimentation in their early years, to provide them with regular and systematic instruction on matters of temperance, especially sobriety and to prepare the more generous and reliable to become members of our Association. It has been found that many children can grasp the notion of reparation to the Sacred Heart of Jesus and of sacrifice for the sake of others. Thousands of the current membership actually began in this way.

PRAYER OF THE JUVENILE PIONEERS:

In your honour, O Sacred Heart of Jesus, and with the help of your Blessed Mother, I promise not to take any alcoholic drink until I am.......years of age. Grant me, O Lord, Your grace to keep my promise and to consider becoming a Pioneer when I am old enough to do so.

JUNIOR PIONEERS

The Junior section carries on the good work started in the primary school. Nowadays, as the majority of youngsters begin post primary school at around 12 years of age, this section helps them meet the challenges of their new environment. During this period they should learn about the effects of alcohol and habit-forming drugs in the hope that they will be dissuaded from dangerous experimentation. The relatively easy availability of these products adds to the urgency of the work. This section can help strengthen the pledge taken at the time of Confirmation in many dioceses and secure its better observance.

PRAYER OF JUNIOR PIONEERS:

For your greater glory and consolation, O Sacred Heart of Jesus, for your sake to give good example, to practice self-denial, to make reparation to you for the sins of intemperance and for the conversion of excessive drinkers I will abstain for my term as a Junior Pioneer. Moreover, I look forward one day to obtaining life membership if you should graciously call me to it.

YOUNG PIONEERS

The Young Pioneer section is for 15 year olds and over. There is a widespread consensus that this age indicates a significant change in the mentality of the growing person. In ancient Rome it was at 15 that the young citizen could wear the *toga virilis,* a sign of adulthood. In our own day it is considered the age of adulthood for the purposes of sociological surveys. There is also evidence of an alarming increase in the use of drugs at the same age. For this reason, Young Pioneers promise to stay off alcohol until at least 18 and to keep away from drugs for life. Membership of the Young Pioneers is intended to help them develop a healthy life-style and prepare them spiritually, psychologically and emotionally for further important choices to be made on leaving school. As mature young adults of high ideals, they will learn to stand by all their commitments, not only where alcohol and habit-forming drugs are concerned but in all the significant areas of their lives- showing fidelity in marriage, integrity in public life, loyalty to their faith and a concern for justice.

PRAYER OF THE YOUNG PIONEERS:

Lord, for your sake, for the recovery of problem drinkers and victims of substance abuse, to make amends to your Sacred Heart for the intemperance in all our lives, I promise not to take alcoholic drink until I am at least 18 (or older, if appropriate) and to keep off drugs for life.

UPLIFTING HYMNS

The one who sings prays twice. *(St Augustine)*

The neighbours of Venerable Matt Talbot, one of the great glories of the Pioneer Association, said that they occasionally heard him singing hymns in his room " in a sweet tenor voice". Matt knew that hymn-singing is not simply an aesthetic link between acts of devotion in a public place of worship. To sing a hymn with faith is itself a highly commendable act of devotion. We list a few hymns here that may be used to nourish devotion, both in private and public.

1. SWEET HEART OF JESUS
Sweet Heart of Jesus, fount of love and mercy,
Today we come Thy blessing to implore;
Oh, touch our hearts, so cold and so ungrateful,
And make them, Lord, Thine own for evermore.
Sweet Heart of Jesus ! we implore,
Oh, make us love Thee more and more.

Sweet Heart of Jesus ! make us know and love Thee,
Unfold to us the treasures of Thy grace,
That so our hearts from things of earth uplifted,
May long alone to gaze upon Thy face. Sweet Heart, etc.

Sweet Heart of Jesus ! make us pure and gentle,
And teach us how to do Thy blessed will,
To follow close the prints of Thy dear footsteps,
And when we fall, sweet Heart, oh, love us still. Sweet Heart, etc.

2. AN OFFERING TO THE SACRED HEART
To Thee, O Heart of Jesus!
To Thee our hearts we give.
Help, help us all to love Thee
And serve Thee while we live.
Yes, yes, till life is o'er
And then for evermore,
O Sacred Heart of Jesus !
We'll love thee and adore.

No heart can be so tender,
No heart can love like Thee.
Thy life-blood all, O Jesus !
Was shed to set us free,
Yes, yes, till life is o'er etc.
Father Russell, S.J.

3. HYMN TO THE BLESSED SACRAMENT
Jesus, my Lord, my God, my all;
How can I love Thee as I ought,
And how revere this wondrous gift,
So far surpassing hope or thought ?
Sweet Sacrament, we Thee adore
O make us love Thee more and more.

Had I but Mary's sinless heart
To love Thee with, my dearest King;
Oh, with what bursts of fervent praise
Thy goodness, Jesus, would I sing !
Sweet Sacrament, etc.
Bishop Chadwick.

4. IN PRAISE OF THE SACRED HEART

To Jesus' Heart, all burning
With fervent love for men,
My heart, with fondest yearning,
Shall raise its joyful strain.
While ages course along,
Blest be with loudest song
The Sacred Heart of Jesus,
By every heart and tongue.
The Sacred Heart of Jesus
By every heart and tongue

As thou art meek and lowly
and ever pure of heart
so may my heart be wholly
of thine the counterpart
When life away is flying
and earth's false glare is done
still, Sacred Heart, in dying
I'll say I'm all thine own
still Sacred heart, in dying
I'll say I'm all thine own.
Father Christie, S.J.

5. NEARER MY GOD TO THEE

Nearer, my God, to thee
Nearer to Thee,
E'en though it be a cross
That raiseth me,
Still all my song shall be
Nearer, my God, to Thee
Nearer to Thee. (x2)

Deep in Thy Sacred Heart
Let me abide;
Thou that hast bled for me,
Sorrowed and died.
Sweet shall my weeping be,
Grief surely leading me-
Nearer, my God, to Thee,
Nearer to Thee. (x2)

Friends may depart from me
Night may come down;
Clouds of adversity
Darken and frown;
Still through my tears I'll see
Hope, gently leading me-
Nearer, my God, to Thee,
Nearer to Thee.(x2)
Mrs. Adams.

6. A DEVOUT PRAYER TO JESUS IN THE BLESSED SACRAMENT

Sweet Sacrament Divine,
Hid in Thy earthly home;
Lo ! round thy lowly shrine
With suppliant hearts we come.
Jesus, to Thee our voice we raise
In songs of love and heartfelt praise,
Sweet Sacrament Divine (x2)

Sweet Sacrament of peace,
Dear home of every heart,
Where restless yearnings cease
And sorrows all depart.
Here in Thy ear all trustfully
We tell our tale of misery,
Sweet Sacrament of Peace. (x2)

Sweet Sacrament of rest,
Ark from the ocean's roar,
Within Thy shelter blest,
Soon may we reach the shore.
Save us, for still the tempest raves,
Save, lest we sink beneath the waves,
Sweet Sacrament of rest. (x2)
Fr Stanfield.

7. SOUL OF MY SAVIOUR

Soul of my Saviour, sanctify my breast,
Body of Christ, be Thou my saving Guest,
Blood of my Saviour,
bathe me in Thy tide,
Wash me, ye waters,
streaming from His side!

Strength and protection may His Passion be;
O Blessed Jesus, hear and answer me !
Deep in Thy Wounds, Lord, hide and
shelter me;
So shall I never, never part from Thee.

Guard and defend me from
the foe malign;
In death's drear moments make
me only Thine;
Call me and bid me come to Thee on high
Where I may praise Thee with
Thy saints for aye.
14th Century

8. A PRAYER FOR MERCY

God of mercy and compassion
Look with pity upon me;
Father, let me call you Father,
'Tis Thy child returns to Thee.
Jesus Lord, I ask for mercy,
Let me not implore in vain;
All my sins I now detest them,
Never will I sin again.

By my sins I have deserved
Death and endless misery;
Hell with all its pains and torments,
And for all eternity.
Jesus, Lord etc.

Fr Vaughan,
C.SS.R.

9. O SACRED HEAD SURROUNDED

O sacred head surrounded
by crown of piercing thorn
O bleeding head so wounded
reviled and put to scorn
Our sins have marred the glory
of thy most holy face
Yet angel hosts adore thee
and tremble as they gaze

The Lord of every nation
was hung upon a tree
his death was our salvation
our sins, his agony.
O Jesus by thy Passion
thy life in us increase
thy death for us did fashion
our pardon and our peace.

J.S. Bach

10. HAIL QUEEN OF HEAVEN

Hail Queen of Heaven, the ocean star
guide of the wanderer here below
thrown on life's surge, we claim thy care
save us from peril and from woe
Mother of Christ, star of the sea
pray for the wanderer, pray for me.

O gentle, chaste and spotless maid
we sinners make our prayers through
thee

remind thy Son that he has paid
the price of our iniquity
Virgin most pure, star of the sea
pray for the sinner, pray for me.

John Lingard (1771-1851)

11. I'LL SING A HYMN TO MARY

I'll sing a hymn to Mary
the mother of my God
the virgin of all virgins
of David's royal blood.
Oh ! teach me, holy Mary,
a loving song to frame,
When wicked men blaspheme thee,
to love and bless thy name.

O Lily of the Valley,
O mystic rose, what tree
or flower e'en the fairest
is half so fair as thee?
O let me though so lowly
recite my mothers fame
When wicked men blaspheme thee
to love and bless thy name.

But in the crown of Mary
there lies a wondrous gem,
As Queen of all the angels,
which Mary shares with them.
"No sin hath e'er defiled thee,"
So doth our faith proclaim;
When wicked men blaspheme thee,
I'll love and bless thy name.

Fr Wyse

12. THE BELLS OF THE ANGELUS

The bells of the angelus call us to pray
in sweet tones announcing the sacred
Ave

Ave,ave,ave Maria
ave,ave, ave Maria

An angel of mercy led Bernadette's feet
where flows a deep torrent Our Lady to
greet. (Chorus)

She prayed to our mother that God's will
be done, she prayed for his glory
that his kingdom come. (Chorus)

13. WHEN CREATION WAS BEGUN

When creation was begun
God had chosen you to be
mother of his blessed Son
Holy Mary, full of grace.

Ave, ave, ave Maria

When creation was restored
you were there beside the Lord
whom you cherished and adored
Holy Mary, full of grace.

Ave, ave, ave Maria

Praise the Father and the Son
and the Spirit, three in one
as it was when time began
now and evermore. Amen.

Ave, ave, ave Maria

14. ALL THAT I AM

All that I am, all that I do,
all that I'll ever have, I offer now to you.
Take and sanctify these gifts
for your honour, Lord,
Knowing that I love and serve you
is enough reward.
All that I am, all that I do,
all that I'll ever have I offer now to you.

All that I dream, all that I pray,
all that I'll ever make, I give to you today.
Take and sanctify these gifts
for your honour, Lord.
Knowing that I love and serve you
is enough reward.
All that I am, all that I do,
all that I'll ever have I offer now to you.

Sebastien Temple

15. WERE YOU THERE WHEN THEY CRUCIFIED MY LORD

1. Were you there when they crucified
   my Lord ?(x2)
   Oh, sometimes it causes me to
   tremble, tremble, tremble.
   Were you there when they crucified
   my Lord?

2. Were you there when they pierced
   him in the side ? (x2)
3. Were you there when the sun refused
   to shine? (x2)
4. Were you there when they laid him in
   the tomb? (x2)
5. Were you there when he rose from out
   the tomb? (x2)

Negro Spiritual

16. BE NOT AFRAID

Be not afraid, I go before you always
Come follow Me and I will give you rest.

1. You shall cross the barren desert,
   but you shall not die of thirst,
   You shall wander far in safety
   though you do not know the way.
   You shall speak your words to foreign
   men
   and they will understand.
   You shall see the face of God
   and live.

2. If you pass through raging waters
   in the sea, you shall not drown.
   If you walk amid the burning flames,
   you shall not be harmed.
   If you stand before the power of hell
   and death is at your side.
   Know that I am with you
   through it all.

3. Blessed are You poor
   for the Kingdom shall be theirs
   Blessed are they that weep and
   mourn
   for one day you shall laugh.
   And if wicked men insult and hate
   you
   all because of Me
   Blessed, blessed are you.

Bob Dufford S.J.

17. LIKE A SHEPHERD HE FEEDS HIS FLOCK

Like a shepherd he feeds his flock
And gathers the lambs in his arms
Holding them carefully close to His heart
Leading them home.

1 Say to the cities of Judah:
Prepare the way of the Lord
Go to the mountaintop, lift your voice;
Jerusalem, here is your God.

2 I myself will shepherd them
For others have led them astray
The lost I will rescue and heal their wounds
And pasture them, giving them rest.

3 Come unto Me
If you are heavily burdened
And take My yoke upon your shoulders
I will give you rest.

Bob Dufford S.J.

18. AG CRIOST AN SIOL

Ag Críost an síol
ag Críost an fómhar.
In iothlain Dé go dtugtar sinn.
Ag Críost an mhuir,
ag Críost an t-íasc
I líonta Dé go gcastar sinn.
Ó fhás go haois,
is ó aois go bás,
Do dhá láimh,
a Chríost, anall tharainn
O bhás go críoch,
ní críoch ach athfhás
i bParthas na nGrást go rabhaimid.

19. CEAD MILE FAILTE ROMHAT

Céad míle fáilte romhat, a Íosa, a Íosa,
Céad míle fáilte romhat, a Íosa,
Céad míle fáilte romhat, a Shlánaitheoir,
Céad míle, mile fáilte romhat, 'Íosa, a Íosa.

Glóir agus moladh duit, a Íosa, a Íosa,
Glóir agus moladh duit, a Íosa.
Glóir agus moladh duit, a Shlánaitheoir,
Glóir, moladh agus buíochas duit,'Íosa, a Íosa.

20. GILE MO CHROI

Gile mo chroí do chroise 'Shlánaitheoir,
Is ciste mo chroí do chroíse d'fháil im chomhair,
Os follas gur líon do chroí dom' ghrás a 'stór,
I gcochall mo chroí do chroíse fág i gcomhad.

Ar fhulaingis trínne a Rí ghil ard na gcomhacht
Ní thuigeann im smaointe a chuiomh na a thrácht i gcóir;
'S gur le goradhghoin nimhe do chroí's do chneasa, a stór,
Do bhrostaigh na mílte saoi go sámh i gcoróin.

A Athair 's a Íosa dhion led bhás mé beo,
'S do dhealbh mo ghnaoi gan chríochnú ceard id chló,
Nach danartha an gníomh, a Chríost, nar ghrása fós,
Ach gach uile ní 'na mbíodh do ghráin don tsórt.

Tadhg Gaelach Ó Súilleabháin

21. BI 'IOSA IM CHROISE

Bí 'Íosa im chroíse 's im chuimhne gach uair,
Bí 'Íosa im chroíse le haithrí go luath,
Bí 'Íosa im chroíse le dúthracht go buan,
'S a Íosa, 'Dhia dhílis, na scar choíche uaim.

'Sé Íosa mo ríse, mo chara 's mo ghrá,
'Sé Íosa mo dhídean ar pheaca 's ar bhás,
'Sé Íosa mo aoibhneas, mo sheasamh de ghnáth,
'S a Íosa, 'Dhia dhílis, na scar liom go bráth.

Bí, 'Íosa, go síoraí im chroí is im bhéal,
Bí, 'Íosa, go síoraí im thuiscint 's im mhéin,
Bí, 'Íosa, go síoraí im mheabhair mar léann,
'S, a Íosa, 'Dhia dhílis, na fág me liom féin.

Traditional Irish

Masses suitable for Pioneer Celebrations

All devotion to the Heart of Jesus and all its manifestations are profoundly Eucharistic. Pope John Paul II, Zakopone, Poland June 6th 1997.

The Votive Mass of the Sacred Heart is most appropriate for a Pioneer Celebration and can be found in the Roman Missal. Provided here are texts of two alternative Pioneer Masses and also a Mass for Temperance suitable for a general congregation.

PIONEER MASS I

Entrance Antiphon
How can I repay the Lord for his goodness to me? I will take the cup of salvation; I will call on God's name. Psalm 115

Opening Prayer
God our Heavenly Father, all that is good, all that is perfect comes to us from you. Spread among us the virtue of temperance that we may use wisely all your other gifts. We ask this through Christ our Lord.

First Reading
A reading from the Epistle to the Ephesians 5, 15 -20

So be very careful about the sort of lives you lead, like intelligent and not like senseless people. This may be a wicked age but your lives should redeem it. And do not be thoughtless but recognise what is the will of the Lord. Do not drug yourselves with wine, this is simply dissipation; be filled with the Spirit. Sing the words and tunes of the psalms when you are together, and go on singing and chanting to the Lord in your hearts, so that always and everywhere you are giving thanks to God who is our Father in the name of Our Lord Jesus Christ.
This is the word of the Lord.
Thanks be to God.

Responsorial Psalm   Ps 115
Response: *My vows to the Lord I will fulfil before all his people.*

I trusted even when I said:
'I am sorely afflicted'.
And when I said in my alarm:
'No man can be trusted'. (R)

How can I repay the Lord
for his goodness to me?
The cup of salvation I will raise:
I will call on the Lord's name. (R)

Your servant, Lord, your servant am I:
you have loosened my bonds.
A thanksgiving sacrifice I make:
I will call on the Lord's name. (R)

My vows to the Lord I will fulfil
before all his people.
O precious in the eyes of the Lord
is the death of his faithful. (R)

My vows to the Lord I will fulfil
before all his people,
in the courts of the house of the Lord,
in your midst, O Jerusalem. (R)

Gospel Acclamation
Alleluia,alleluia. When he saw him, he had compassion, and went to him and
bound up his wounds. Alleluia.

Gospel
A reading from the Holy Gospel according to Luke (10, 25 - 37)

And now a lawyer stood up and, to test Jesus, asked, 'Master, what must I do
to inherit eternal life?' He said to him,' What is written in the Law? What is
your reading of it?' He replied, ' You must love the Lord your God with all
your heart, with all your soul, with all your strength, and with all your mind,
and your neighbour as yourself.' Jesus said to him,'You have answered right,
do this and life is yours'. But the man was anxious to justify himself and said
to Jesus:
'And who is my neighbour? In answer Jesus said,' A man was once on his
way down from Jerusalem to Jericho and fell into the hands of bandits; they
stripped him, beat him and then made off, leaving him half dead. Now a priest
happened to be travelling down the same road, but when he saw the man, he
passed by on the other side. In the same way a Levite who came to the place
saw him, and passed by on the other side. But a Samaritan traveller who came

on him was moved with compassion when he saw him. He went up to him and bandaged his wounds, pouring oil and wine on them. He then lifted him onto his own mount and took him to an inn and looked after him. Next day, he took out two denarii and handed them to the innkeeper and said," Look after him, and on my way back I will make good any extra expense you have." Which of these three, do you think, proved himself a neighbour to the man who fell into the bandits' hands? He replied, 'The one who showed pity towards him.' Jesus said to him, 'Go, and do the same yourself.'
This is the Gospel of the Lord

Praise to you, Lord Jesus Christ.

Homily.

Blessing and Ceremonies **(See pages 91-92)**

PRAYERS OF THE FAITHFUL: (See page 107)

Members of the Pioneer Association now recite their Offering.

Pioneer Offering:
For Your greater glory and consolation, O Sacred Heart of Jesus, for Your sake to give good example, to practise self-denial, to make reparation to You for the sins of intemperance and for the conversion of excessive drinkers, I will abstain for life from all intoxicating drinks.
Offering composed by Fr. James Cullen, s.j.

Prayer over the gifts
Lord, accept our gifts of bread and wine, poor offerings but rich in what they signify - our offering of ourselves to you. We ask this through Christ Our Lord.

Preface: Choice of celebrant

Communion Verse
Your words are spirit, Lord, and they are life:
You have the message of eternal life.

Prayer after Communion
We who have been nourished by this heavenly food, O God, beg you to bestow your grace on alcoholics and excessive drinkers so that they may overcome the addiction which is the cause of so much suffering and sorrow to themselves and others. We ask this through Christ Our Lord.

PIONEER MASS II

Entrance Antiphon
Come to me all you who labour and are overburdened and I will give you rest.
(Matt.11:28)

Opening Prayer
Lord God, bless the work of the Pioneer Association, strengthen the
commitment of its members and grant them perseverance. Help all of us to
respond generously to the love of the Heart of your Son so that we may bring
that love to those around us.
We ask this through Christ our Lord.

First Reading
A Reading from the prophet Isaiah 41:9-10,13-14

The Lord said this: You whom I brought from the confines of the earth and
called from the ends of the world: you to whom I said: I have chosen you, not
rejected you, do not be afraid, for I am with you; stop being anxious and
watchful, for I am your God. I give you strength, I bring you help, I uphold you
with my victorious right hand. I tell you "Do not be afraid, I will help you."
This is the word of the Lord.

Responsorial Psalm
Response: *Remember your mercy, Lord*

1. Lord, make me know your way.
Lord, teach me your paths.
Make me walk in your truth and teach me:
For you are God my Saviour.

2. Remember your mercy, Lord, and the love you have shown from of old.
Do not remember the sins of my youth.
In your love remember me, because of your goodness, O Lord.

3. The Lord is good and upright
He shows the path to those who stray
He guides the humble in the right path,
He teaches His way to the poor.

4. His ways are faithfulness and love for those who keep
His covenant and will.
The Lord's friendship is for those who revere Him
To them He reveals His covenant.

Second Reading
Letter to the Colossians 3:12-15
You are God's chosen race, His saints; He loves you, and you should be clothed in sincere compassion, in kindness and humility, gentleness and patience. Bear with one another; forgive each other as soon as a quarrel begins. The Lord has forgiven you; now you must do the same. Over all these clothes, to keep them together and complete them, put on love. And may the peace of Christ reign in your hearts, because it is for this that you are called together as parts of one body. Always be thankful.
This is the word of the Lord.

Gospel Acclamation
Alleluia, Alleluia I am the Light of the world, says the Lord, anyone who follows me will have the light of life, Alleluia.

Gospel
A reading from the holy Gospel according to Matthew 22:35-40

A lawyer, to disconcert Jesus, put a question: "Master, which is the greatest commandment of the law?" Jesus said: "You must love the Lord with all your heart, with all your soul and with all your mind. This is the greatest and the first commandment. The second resembles it: You must love your neighbour as yourself. On these two commandments hang the whole law and the prophets also."
This is the Gospel of the Lord.

Praise to you, Lord Jesus Christ.

Homily.

Blessing and Ceremonies **(See pages 91-92)**

PRAYERS OF THE FAITHFUL: (See page 107)

Pioneer Offering:
For Your greater glory and consolation, O Sacred Heart of Jesus, for Your sake to give good example, to practise self-denial, to make reparation to You for the sins of intemperance and for the conversion of excessive drinkers, I will abstain for life from all intoxicating drinks.
Offering composed by Fr. James Cullen, s.j.

Prayer over the gifts
Father of Mercy, hear our prayers for those who have become over-dependent on alcohol. Give them the grace of determination and perseverance in their struggle to overcome their dependence and to live fully to the glory of God.
We ask this through Christ our Lord.

Preface: Mass of the Sacred Heart.

Communion Antiphon
May your love be upon us, O Lord, as we place all our hope in you.

Prayer after Communion
Lord God, look with compassion on the relatives of those with drink problems. Give them courage and patience so that they will be able to overcome the difficulties in their lives. Lift up their hearts so that they do not despair but always cherish a spirit of hope.
We ask this through Christ Our Lord.

Alternative Readings suitable for either Pioneer Masses I or II

A reading from the prophet Ezekiel 36:25-28

I shall pour clean water over you and you will be cleansed. I shall give you a new heart, and put a new spirit in you; I shall remove the heart of stone from your bodies and give you a heart of flesh instead. I shall put my spirit in you, and make you keep my laws and sincerely respect my observances. You shall be my people and I will be your God.

A reading from the letter of St. Paul to the Philippians 1:8-11

God knows how much I miss you all, loving you as Jesus Christ loves you. My prayer is that your love for each other may increase more and more and never stop improving your knowledge and deepening your perception so that you can always recognise what is best.
This will help you to become pure and blameless, and prepare you for the day of Christ when you will reach the perfect goodness which Jesus Christ produces in us for the glory and praise of God.

A reading from the Holy Gospel according to John. 15:9-17

Jesus said to His disciples: As the Father has loved me so I have loved you. Remain in my love. If you keep my commandments, you will remain in my love, just as I have kept my Father's commandments and remain in His love. I have told you this so that my own joy may be in you and your joy be complete. This is my commandment: love one another as I have loved you. A man can have no greater love than to lay down his life for his friends. You are my friends if you do what I command you. I shall not call you servants any more because a servant does not know his master's business; I call you friends because I have made known to you everything I have learned from my Father. You did not choose me, no, I chose you and I commissioned you to go out and bear fruit, fruit that will last, and then the Father will give you anything that you ask in my name. What I command you is to love one another.

MASS FOR TEMPERANCE

Entrance Antiphon
Always be joyful, then, in the Lord: I repeat, be joyful. Let your good sense be obvious to everybody. The Lord is near (Philippians 4, 4-5)

Opening Prayer.
Heavenly Father, while on earth Your Son shared both the innocent pleasure of Cana and the painful privation of the desert. May the example of His perfect humanity guide us through the ever-changing situations of life. We ask this through Our Lord Jesus Christ Your Son who lives and reigns with You and the Holy Spirit One God forever and ever.

First Reading
A Reading from the Letter to the Galatians (5,18-26)

Let me put it to you like this. If you are guided by the Spirit you will be in no danger of yielding to self-indulgence, since self-indulgence is the opposite of the Spirit, the Spirit is totally against such a thing, and it is precisely because the two are so opposed that you do not always carry out your good intentions. If you are led by the Spirit, no law can touch you.

This is the word of the Lord.
Thanks be to God.

Response: A pure heart create for me O God.
Have mercy on me, O God in your kindness.
In your compassion blot out my offence.
O wash me more and more from my guilt
and cleanse me from my sin. (R)

My offences truly I know them
my sin is always before me.
Against you, you alone, have I sinned;
what is evil in your sight I have done. (R)

A pure heart create for me, O God
Put a steadfast spirit within me.
Do not cast me away from your presence,
nor deprive me of your holy spirit. (R)

Give me again the joy of your help;
with a spirit of fervour sustain me,
that I may teach transgressors your ways
and sinners may return to you. (R)

Gospel Acclamation
Alleluia, Alleluia nothing that goes into someone from outside can make that person unclean, Alleluia.

GOSPEL

A reading from the Holy Gospel according to Mark. (7,14-23)
Jesus called the people to himself again and said "Listen to me, all of you, and understand.   Nothing that goes into someone from outside can make that person unclean; it is the things that come out of someone that make that person unclean. Those who have ears to hear, let them listen to this".
When he had gone back into the house, away from the crowd, his disciples questioned him about the parable. He said to them, "Do you not understand either? Can you not see that whatever goes into someone from outside cannot make that person unclean, because it does not go into the heart but through the stomach and passes out into the sewer?" (Thus he pronounced all foods clean). And he went on, "It is what comes out of someone that makes a person unclean.   For it is from within, from the heart, that evil intentions emerge: fornication, theft, murder, adultery, avarice, malice, deceit, indecency, envy, slander, pride, folly.   All these things come from within and make a person unclean.

This is the Gospel of the Lord.
Praise to you, Lord Jesus Christ.

Homily.

PRAYERS OF THE FAITHFUL: (See page 107)

Prayer over the Gifts
Almighty Father, we now offer to you bread and wine from the store you have given us.   Through the work of your grace, may we always be ready to share the one and moderate our use of the other.   Through Christ Our Lord.

Preface: Choice of Celebrant

Communion Verse
Your words are spirit, Lord, and they are life:
You have the message of eternal life.

Prayer after Communion
Lord, the Heart of Your Son was once moved at the sight of those who suffered through lack of life's necessities.   Let us share deeply in that compassion and vigorously give it expression in our lives.   Through the same Christ Our Lord.

PRAYERS OF THE FAITHFUL

As a rule the sequence of intentions in these prayers is : a) for the needs of the Church, b) for public authorities and the salvation of the world,c) for those oppressed by any need, d) for the local community. In particular celebrations, such as a Pioneer initiation, renewal or jubilee ceremony, the list of intentions may be more closely concerned with the special occasion. cf General Instructions of the Roman Missal. Nos 45,46,47.

A selection may be made from among the following prayers some of which are based directly on the wording of the Pioneer Offering.

Priest: As we gather round the altar, let renew our promise to the Sacred Heart and confide all our cares to his tender mercy.
or
The Lord is merciful and always ready to help us start again. Let us pray for the generosity and self-control to do his will.
or
Trusting in God's goodness and conscious of our own weakness, we confess our shortcomings and ask for His special help.

1. Lord, you invite each one of us to glorify and console Your Sacred Heart by freely denying ourselves the use of one of Your gifts. May this renunciation prepare our own hearts to receive the even greater gifts You promise to those who love You. **Lord Hear Us.**

2. Lord, who alone are good, guide our members to live out their commitment sincerely, so that their efforts may truly glorify You and be an encouraging example to others. **Lord Hear Us.**

3. Lord, You have told us that only those who take up their cross each day and follow you can consider themselves your disciples; help us to honour our commitment totally, generously and cheerfully. **Lord Hear Us.**

4. Lord, you came to raise a fallen world and to heal the wounds of our sins. Allow us to share in Your work of reparation for our own sins of self-indulgence and the sins of those who drink to excess. **Lord Hear Us.**

5. Lord, touch the hearts of excessive drinkers, let them feel the futility of their ways and console those whom You ask to share their lives. **Lord Hear Us.**

6. Comfort innocent victims of excessive drinking, especially children and those injured in accidents. **Lord Hear Us.**

7. Guide those engaged in the licensed trade to act conscientiously for the common good. **Lord Hear Us.**

8. Bless abundantly the efforts of workers in research, prevention and care of alcoholism and drug abuse. **Lord Hear Us.**

9. Let us ask the Lord to give comfort and hope to those who live with an immoderate drinker or addict and who are subject to stress and suffering. **Lord Hear Us.**

10. Let us pray that, weak as we know we are, we will, with His help, make up for intemperances of the past, including our own. **Lord Hear Us.**

11. Let us pray that the Lord, who sees the sin and suffering caused by excessive drinking and drug abuse, will bless our efforts to lessen abuse and promote the virtue of sobriety. **Lord Hear Us.**

12. Let us ask the Lord to inspire many men and women, girls and boys, to join our Association and serve Him generously as Pioneers. **Lord Hear Us.**

13. We ask for light and grace to bring our conduct into line with faith we are privileged to profess...**Lord Hear Us.**

14. May our children find our conduct worthy of imitation...**Lord Hear Us.**

15. Help young people to avoid dangerous experimentation with drink and drugs. **Lord Hear Us.**

16. Make us aware of the serious implications of drinking and driving. **Lord Hear Us.**

17. God is glorified in his saints. Let us pray for the canonisation of Venerable Matt Talbot, Venerable Edel Quinn, the Servants of God, Fr John Sullivan and Frank Duff, all members of the Pioneer Association. **Lord Hear Us.**

18. Let us pray for deceased members of the Pioneer Association, especially........................... **Lord Hear Us.**

19. Let us pray silently for someone in particular. **Lord Hear Us.**

20. Let us pray silently for our own private intentions. **Lord Hear Us.**

Priest: Lord, it is our sincere intention to be constant in your service. Grant us forgiveness for our failings and assist us to be living witnesses of our faith. We ask this through Christ our Lord

or

O God, protector of those who trust in you, through the special intercession of Mary, guide of all wanderers, grant that we may so use the good things of time that we may not lose those that are eternal. Through Christ our Lord.

Where appropriate, members may now be invited to recite aloud together the words of the Pioneer Offering.

For your greater glory and consolation, O Sacred Heart of Jesus, for Your sake to give good example, to practice self-denial, to make reparation to You for the sins of intemperance and for the conversion of excessive drinkers, I will abstain for life from all intoxicating drinks.

Offering composed by Fr James Cullen, S.J.

Appendices

From the autobiography and letters of St Margaret Mary Alacoque

APPENDIX A

I believe that the reason behind our Lord's great desire that especial honour should be paid to his Sacred Heart is his wish to renew in our souls the effects of our redemption. For his Sacred Heart is an inexhaustible spring which has no other purpose than to overflow into hearts which are humble, so that they may be ready and willing to devote their lives to his goodwill and pleasure.

Out of this divine heart three streams gush forth uninterruptedly. The first stream is one of mercy for sinners to whom it brings in its flow the spirit of contrition and penance. The second stream is one of charity which flows to bring help to all those who are labouring under difficulties and especially to those who are aspiring after perfection, that all may find support in overcoming difficulties. But the third stream flows with love and light to those who are Christ's perfect friends, who he wishes to bring to complete union with himself, to share with them his own knowledge and commandments, so that they may give themselves up entirely, each in his own way, to enhancing Christ's glory.

APPENDIX B

This divine heart is an ocean full of all good things wherein poor souls can cast all their needs; it is an ocean full of joy to drown all our sadness, an ocean of humility to overwhelm our folly, an ocean of mercy for those in distress, an ocean of love in which to submerge our poverty.

Unite yourself, therefore, to the heart of our Lord Jesus Christ; when you first turn to him so that you may do well, and when you have turned to him so that you may make satisfaction for sin. Do you find that you are making no progress in prayer? Let it be enough for you to offer to God the prayer which our Saviour makes for us in the most holy sacrament of the altar, using his fervent offering to make reparation for your own lukewarmness. And whenever you do anything pray in this way: 'My God, I am going to do this or endure that in the Sacred Heart of your divine Son and according to his holy intentions which I offer you to make reparation for whatever evil or imperfection there may be in my own deeds.' Continue in this way in all the circumstances of life. And whenever anything happens to you that is painful, hard to bear or mortifying, tell yourself this: 'Accept what the Sacred Heart of Jesus sends you in order to unite you to himself..'

But above all things maintain peace of heart which surpasses every treasure. For maintaining this peace nothing is more effective than to renounce one's own will and to set in its place the will of the Sacred Heart, so that he may do for us whatever redounds to his glory and that we may joyfully submit to him and place in him our full confidence.

APPENDIX C
MYSTIC AND TEACHER OF PRAYER
St Margaret Mary was ordered under obedience to reveal something of her extraordinary interior life. As a person of deep humility she found this repugnant but since she considered obedience paramount she complied. She recounted a telling incident from her first days as a Visitation nun.

"When I asked the novice-mistress to teach me to pray, which I had such a hunger to do, she wouldn't believe that having come into religion at 23 years of age, I didn't know how to do it. When I convinced her that I didn't she said to me, "Go and put yourself before the Lord like a canvas before a painter". I wanted her to explain what she meant, as I didn't understand what she was talking about, but I didn't dare say it. Then I heard someone say, " Come and I will teach you".

When I got to prayer, my Sovereign Master made me see that my soul was the canvas on which he wished to paint all the features of his life of suffering which was lived out in love and privation, separation, silence and sacrifice, in its consummation. And that he himself would do the painting after having purified my soul of all the stains that remained, both of earthly attachments and love of myself and creatures, to which I was naturally attracted. At that very instant he despoiled me of everything, and after having emptied my heart and left my soul completely naked, he enkindled in me such a burning desire to love him and suffer that it gave me no rest, pursuing me so closely that I could think of nothing else except how I could love him in crucifying myself; and his goodness to me has always been so great that he has never failed to provide me with the means to make this a reality.

APPENDIX D
THE DOUBLE PICTURE OF A HAPPY LIFE AND OF A CRUCIFIED LIFE.
One time this unique Love of my soul presented himself before me carrying on one hand a painting depicting the most happy life that one could imagine for a religious soul, filled with peace, full of interior and exterior consolations, a perfect health as well as the approbation and esteem of everybody and other things very delightful to human nature. On the other hand he carried a picture of a totally different sort of life, this time poor and miserable, continually crucified by all sorts of humiliations, rejections, contradictions, suffering the whole time in body and mind. In presenting these pictures he said to me: "Choose, my daughter, the one that you find the most agreeable and I will guarantee you the same graces for one as for the other". I knelt down before him in adoration, saying: "Lord, I want nothing but you and the choice you make for me". After he had urged me strongly to choose, "You are enough for me, My God. Do for me whatever glorifies you the most, without regard for my interests or satisfactions. Content yourself and that will do me". Then he said that, with Mary Magdalen, I

had chosen the better part which would never be taken from me because he would be my heritage forever. In giving me the painting of crucifixion, "Here", he said, "is what I have chosen and which is most acceptable to me, both for the accomplishment of my plans as for making you like me. The other is the way of pleasure, not of merits: it is for eternity."

I then accepted this picture of death and crucifixion by kissing the hand that offered it to me; and although my nature recoiled I embraced it with all the affection of my heart and in pressing it close to my breast I felt it so strongly imprinted in me, that I seemed to form a unit with all I had seen represented.

APPENDIX E
VISION OF 1688

In the following letter written by St Margaret Mary in 1688, two years before her death, to her former superior Mother de Saumaise she records one of her visions. Few private letters have ever had a bigger impact on Catholic piety. For the members of the Society of Jesus, this letter has been accepted as the basis of their involvement in promoting Sacred Heart devotion and known to them as their <u>munus suavissimum</u> (delightful responsibility). The promises made in the vision, however, have always been understood as on offer, not only to Visitation nuns and Jesuit priests, but to all men and women who want to make the Sacred Heart known and loved.

It is out of obedience to my Sovereign, dear Mother, that I shall try, when He permits it, to satisfy in all simplicity the request you make that I tell you of His continued mercies and generosity to me. They are so great that often they make me simply exclaim: *Misericordias Domini in aeternum cantabo!* (I will sing forever of the mercies of the Lord) Alas, what else could I say, when my heart is so full I cannot express myself? I am surrounded by His blessings on every side, I am so buried in them I cannot escape. I feel myself to be a little drop of water in this ocean of the Sacred Heart. It is an abyss of every good, an inexhaustible source of every delight. The more one draws from it the more abundantly it flows. It is a hidden and infinite treasure which asks only to show itself to us, to diffuse and distribute itself to enrich our poverty. I value it and love it more than all His gifts, graces and benefactions. I let Him act in me, with me, for me, according to His good pleasure. I take no notice of anything but Him. He is worth a million times more than all else besides. If you did not oblige me to write you something about this I should leave everything in Him who makes me powerless to say anything except to those He wishes me to. You are one of these.

I must tell you that I had the good fortune of spending all day on the feast of the Visitation *(In those days, July 2nd)* before the Blessed Sacrament. My Sovereign deigned to favour His wretched slave with several special graces from His loving Heart. He drew me into Himself and made me experience things I cannot express. He showed me a very high place, spacious and wonderfully beautiful, in the midst of which was set up a throne of flames and within it the lovable Heart of Jesus with Its wound. From this shot forth flames so luminous and glowing that the whole place was lighted up and warmed by them. The

Blessed Virgin was on one side and Saint Francis de Sales and the saintly Father de la Colombière on the other. The Daughters of the Visitation were there with their guardian angels beside them, each one holding a heart in his hand. The Blessed Virgin invited us with these words: "Come, my well-beloved daughters, draw near, for I want to make you the trusted guardians of this precious treasure which the divine Sun of justice formed within the virginal soil of my heart, where It lay hidden nine months. After that It was manifested to men. But they did not recognise Its value and contemned It because they saw It mixed and covered with the clay of their humanity. Onto It the Eternal Father had cast all the filth and corruption of our sins. These He caused to be purified away for thirty-three years by the burning flames of Its charity. But seeing that men, far from enriching themselves and making use of so precious a treasure for the purpose for which It was given them but rather trying to set It at naught and exterminate It, if possible, from the face of the earth, the Eternal Father, by an excess of mercy, made use of their malice only to render yet more useful this precious gold. By the blows they gave It in His Passion they have made of It priceless money, stamped with the image of the divinity, so that with It they might pay their debts and carry on the great business of their eternal salvation."

This Queen of goodness continued to speak. She said to them, pointing to this Divine Heart: " This is the precious treasure especially revealed to you because of the tender love my Son has for your Institute. He loves it and considers it His dear Benjamin, and for that reason wants you to have a greater share in this inheritance than all the others. They must not only enrich themselves with this treasure but do all they can to put this precious money in circulation. They must distribute it lavishly, trying to enrich the whole world with it without fear of depleting it. For the more of it they take the more of it there will be left to take."

Then turning to the good Father de la Colombière *(who had died six years earlier in 1682)* this Mother of goodness said: " As for you, faithful servant of My divine Son, you have a great share in this precious Treasure. For if it is given the Daughters of the Visitation to know and distribute it to others, it is reserved to the Fathers of your Society to show and make known its utility and value so that people may profit from It by receiving It with the respect and gratitude due so great a benefit. In proportion as they give Him this pleasure, this divine Heart, source of blessings and graces, will shower them so abundantly on the works of their ministry that they will produce fruits far beyond their labours and expectations. And this, too, for their own personal salvation and perfection."

Our holy founder, *(St Francis de Sales)* speaking to his daughters, said to them: "Esteemed daughters, come and draw from the source of all blessings the waters of salvation. From it a little rivulet, your Constitutions, has already flowed forth into your souls. In this Divine Heart you will find an easy way of acquitting yourselves perfectly of what is enjoined you in the first article of your Directory. This contains in substance the whole perfection of your Institute, and reads; 'Let their whole life and endeavour tend to unite them with God.' For that end let this Sacred Heart be the life that animates us and His love our continual exercise. This alone can unite us with God, help holy Church by prayer and good example, and further the salvation of our neighbour. With this in view, let us pray in the Heart and through the Heart of Jesus, Which wishes henceforth to make Itself the Mediator between God and man. Our good example shall consist in living in conformity with the holy maxims and virtues of this Divine Heart and we shall further the salvation of our neighbour by spreading among them this holy devotion. Let us try to diffuse the good odour of the Sacred Heart of Jesus Christ into the hearts of the faithful, so that we may become the joy and crown of this lovable Heart."

Thereupon all the guardian angels drew near to present Him with what they held in their hands. As soon as these hearts touched the sacred wound they became beautiful and shone like stars. Some of them did not shine as brightly as others. The names of several remained written in letters of gold in the Sacred Heart, into Which some of those I speak of eagerly disappeared and were buried with mutual pleasure. These words were spoken: "In this abyss of love is your dwelling place and repose forever." These were the hearts of those who had laboured the most to make him known and loved. Yours, I think, dear Mother, was among them.

I shall not explain what I heard about the others for this letter is already too long, and besides I think you understand well enough. I shall simply add that the Divine Heart will reward not only you personally but your relatives as well. He looks on them with an eye of mercy and will help them in all their needs provided only they approach Him with confidence. He will remember forever all they do for His glory.

APPENDIX F

The twelve promises of the Sacred Heart revealed at different times to the Saint and gleaned from her writings.

1. I will give them all the graces necessary in their state of life.
2. I will establish peace in their homes.
3. I will comfort them in all their afflictions
4. I will be their secure refuge during life, and above all in death.
5. I will bestow abundant blessings upon all their undertakings.
6. Sinners shall find in My Heart the source and infinite ocean of mercy.
7. Tepid souls shall become fervent.
8. Fervent souls shall quickly mount to high perfection.
9. I will bless every place in which an image of My Heart shall be exposed and honoured.
10. I will give to priests the gift of touching the most hardened hearts.
11. Those who shall promote this devotion shall have their names written in My Heart, never to be effaced.
12. I promise you in the excessive mercy of My Heart that My all-powerful love will grant to all those who communicate on the First Friday in nine consecutive months the grace of final penitence; they shall not die outside My grace nor without receiving their Sacraments. My Divine Heart shall be their safe refuge in this last moment.

Bibliography

Arrupe, Pedro. SJ. *Rooted and Grounded in Love*, Gujarat Sahitya Prakash, Anand - Gujarat 1981

Bainvel, Jean V. SJ. *Devotion to the Sacred Heart*, London: Burns and Oates, 1924

Bougaud, Emile. *Life of St. Margaret Mary Alacoque*, New York, Benziger Bros. 1920. Reprinted Tan Books, Rockford Illinois 1990.

Croiset, Jean. SJ. *The Devotion to the Sacred Heart of Our Lord Jesus Christ*, Translated by Patrick O'Connell. John English and Co., Wexford 1948

Darricau, Raymond. *Vie et oeuvres de Sainte Marguerite- Marie*, 2 vols. Editions Saint-Paul, Paris-Fribourg 1990

Gallifet, Joseph de. SJ. *L'Excellence de la Devotion Adorable de Jesus - Christ*, Montreuil-sur-Mer, Imprimerie Notre Dame des Pres 1897

Guitton, Georges. S.J. *Perfect Friend (Life of St Claude)*, St Louis: B. Herder Co., 1956.

Hamon, A. SJ. *Histoire de la Devotion au Sacré-Coeur*, 5 vols. Paris: Gabriel Beauchesne et Cie 1923-39

Larkin, Francis. SS.CC. *Enthronement of the Sacred Heart*, Daughters of St Paul, Boston 1978

Mac Gréil, Micheál SJ. *Towards a Second Century*, Pioneer Association, Dublin 1993

McKenna, Lambert SJ., *Rev James A Cullen SJ.*, Longmans, Green and Co. London 1924

O'Rahilly, Alfred. *Fr William Doyle SJ.*, Longmans Green and Co. London 1925

O'Donnell, Timothy T. *Heart of the Redeemer*, San Francisco: Ignatius Press 1989 (contains a comprehensive bibliography on Devotion to the Sacred Heart)

Purcell, Mary, *Remembering Matt Talbot*, Veritas, Dublin 1990.

Stierli, Joseph, SJ. *Heart of the Saviour*, A symposium on Devotion to the Sacred Heart. Edited by J. Stierli. Translated by Paul Andrews S.J. Herder and Herder New York and Thomas Nelson and Sons Ltd Edinburgh and London 1957.